CLOUDS

First presented by the Hampstead Theatre Club at the Hampstead Theatre, London, on August 16th, 1976, with the following cast:

Owen	Nigel Hawthorne
Mara	Barbara Ferris
Ed	James Berwick
Angel	Paul Chapman
Hilberto	Olu Jacobs

Directed by Michael Rudman

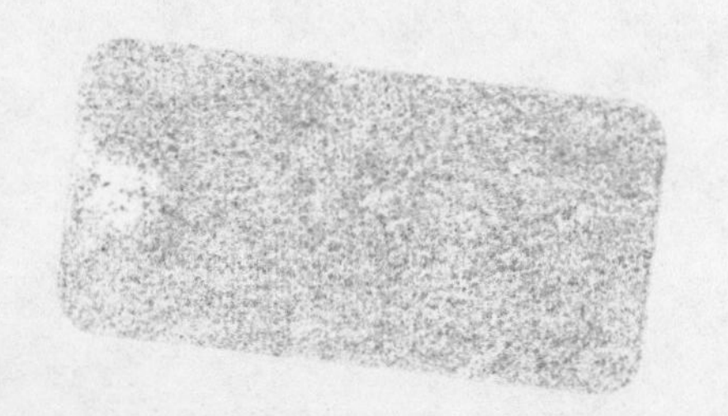

ACT I

Scene 1

Cuba

Or, at any rate, an empty blue sky. Beneath it, the stage offers a simple arrangement of slightly different levels, some of them making a step high enough to be sat upon

Six chairs and a table. The table is arranged as a desk, with one of the chairs behind it, and another in front, sideways on, waiting for visitors. The other four chairs are arranged in a row at one side, as in a waiting-room

Owen is standing by the visitor's chair, in front of the desk. He is a middle-aged man who has been a professional journalist all his life, and who has adopted a sceptical character to protect himself from his own profound susceptibility. He is wearing an open-necked shirt and no jacket. He is also curiously bent over, with his head twisted downwards and sideways. This is because he is trying to read, upside down, the papers on the desk; something that becomes clear when he straightens up, looks round to make sure that he is unobserved, and edges discreetly round to the other side of the desk to read the papers the right way up

Enter Mara. She is in her thirties, and is subject to moods which shift from brilliant vitality to inert melancholia. At the moment she is in the former phase

Mara *¡Buenos dias!*
Owen Ah. Good morning!

He picks up a fan and fans himself, to explain his presence on the wrong side of the desk

Mara (*enunciates carefully*) I am late.
Owen (*likewise*) I am hot.
Mara I sit outside.
Owen I come in here.
Mara I close my eyes in the sunlight.

Owen I find no-one.
Mara I cannot move.
Owen Now I am cool.
Mara Please forgive me.
Owen *Buenos dias.*
Mara *Buenos dias.*

They shake hands

I sit on the Malecon, with the sea on one side, and the white towers of the city on the other, and my head is full of light.
Owen My head also.
Mara And now at last on such a day I believe it: all things are possible.
Owen I believe it also.
Mara Under such a sky, civilizations commence. In Egypt. In Greece.
Owen Now here in Cuba!
Mara And you speak English.
Owen I speak English. (*He draws out the chair behind the desk for her*) Please!
Mara (*gesturing to him to take the place himself*) Oh, please, please!
Owen No, no!
Mara Yes, yes! (*Smilingly indicating the visitor's chair in front of the desk*) I—here!
Owen (*smilingly accepting this arrangement*) Very well. Then I—here! (*He draws up one of the four waiting chairs, so that they are both sitting on equal terms in front of the desk*)
Mara I am happy to be here in Cuba.
Owen Good. I also am happy to be here in Cuba.
Mara I am happy that you are happy.
Owen In my country, we hear many lies about your country.
Mara With us, the same.
Owen Yes?
Mara I think that is not good.
Owen No, not good.
Mara I think that is bad.
Owen Very bad!
Mara Bad, bad, bad!
Owen I am here to tell the truth.
Mara Good! I also!

Owen I want to tell it like it is!
Mara Yes! That is good! To tell it like it is!
Owen It is an expression we have.
Mara We too!
Owen Yes?
Mara Yes!
Owen Then we tell it like it is—together!
Mara That is how people should always be.
Owen We show them how to do it.
Mara You speak English very well!
Owen (*laughing at the joke*) You too!
Mara (*laughing*) Yes?
Owen Yes!
Mara We shall get on well, then!
Owen Very well! Very, very well! I feel it!
Mara I also!
Owen Your country is famous for its beautiful women!
Mara Yes?
Owen Yes! Now I see it with my own eyes!
Mara People say that the men in your country are very passionate! Is that so?
Owen We have a certain dogged persistence that seems to go down quite well in some quarters.
Mara (*her special manner disappears abruptly*) You're English.
Owen And full of dogged persistence!
Mara Oh God.
Owen Sorry?
Mara Is there anything worse than speaking a foreign language to someone who turns out to be English? Yes—speaking English to them very slowly and distinctly.
Owen (*his special manner evaporates, too*) You mean you're . . . You're not . . . Are you English?
Mara Of course I'm English.
Owen Oh God.
Mara Not a good start.
Owen I'm sorry. I just assumed . . .
Mara Naturally.
Owen If you're in Cuba, and you have an appointment with someone in the Ministry of External Relations, you naturally take if for granted that they're . . .

Mara Of course.
Owen I'm sorry.
Mara Please.
Owen Obviously, if you stop and think about it, there's no reason why the Cuban Government shouldn't have English people working for it.
Mara Who's working for the Cuban Government? You're working for the Cuban Government?
Owen *I'm* not working for the Cuban Government. I assume *you're* working for the Cuban Government.
Mara *I'm* not working for the Cuban Government.
Owen You mean . . . you're just waiting for the bloke who deals with the press?
Mara Obviously.
Owen I see.
Mara You're also just waiting for the bloke who deals with the press?
Owen Obviously.
Mara I was supposed to see him at eleven.
Owen I was supposed to see him at eleven. They rang me at the hotel this morning.
Mara They rang me at the hotel this morning.
Owen I must say, I didn't realize it was going to be some great press jamboree for all and sundry.
Mara No, the message I got said nothing about a jamboree.
Silence

Owen You arrived last night, did you? On the flight from Madrid?
Mara There weren't any other flights.
Owen I didn't see you on the plane.
Mara I didn't see you.
Owen I haven't seen you on these jobs before.
Mara I'm not a journalist.
Owen You're not a journalist?
Mara Why should I be a journalist?
Owen Well, I naturally assumed . . . It seemed reasonable to suppose . . . But you're not?
Mara I'm not.
Silence

Owen So what are you, then?
Mara I write books.
Owen Books? What kind of books?
Mara Oblong books.
Owen Novels?
Mara Obviously.
Owen Have I heard of you?
Mara Oh God.
Owen No, I mean, tell me your name
Mara Hill.
Owen Susan Hill?
Mara No.
Owen Lucienne Hill?
Mara Lavender Hill.
Owen *Lavender* Hill?
Mara Mara Hill.
Owen Mara Hill . . . Mara Hill . . . Mara Hill . . .
Mara Don't keep saying it. Each time you say it, it sounds more unreal.
Owen Tell me some titles.

Mara sighs

Go on.
Mara (*looking at her watch*) What's happened to him?
Owen I may have heard of them.
Mara He said eleven.
Owen I can't see any point in being coy about it.
Mara It must be ninety in here.

Silence

Owen *To Where I Lay Dying*. Yes?
Mara Yes.
Owen You see?
Mara See what?
Owen That I've heard of you.
Mara Yes. Good.
Owen Girl on the cover wearing a bridal veil?
Mara Yes.
Owen And nothing else?
Mara Small gold crucifix.

Owen I didn't notice that, I must admit. *To Where I Lay Dying* . . .
Mara Or at any rate *Sighing*.
Owen *Sighing?* She's lying sighing, is she?
Mara Yes.
Owen Not lying dying?
Mara No.
Owen *To Where I Lay Sighing?*
Mara Right.
Owen Nice title. I think my wife may have read it. She's quite keen on that sort of thing.

Silence

To Where I Lay Sighing . . . Dying . . . Dying?
Mara *Sighing*.
Owen *Sighing*. Yes. *To Where I Lay Sighing*.
Mara Please don't keep saying it.
Owen Anyway, you've come to take a look at Cuba. Not a bad idea. Man I was talking to on the plane last night was telling me that the Cubans are a very passionate lot. Surprising amount going on at the weekend in the sugar cane. Might make a rather good setting for your kind of thing. This your first trip?
Mara Yes.
Owen They're all the same, these places. Russia, Egypt, Pakistan —it's all the same kind of set-up. Government car. Guided tour of collective farms and irrigation projects. National folk-dance company. Interview with the Minister of Tourism and Fishmeal Production. Kindergarten where they line up and sing you a patriotic song. Well, look, you go along with it for a couple of days, just to humour them, just so they can't turn round and accuse you of starting off with a hostile attitude. Then you put the boot in. Insist on seeing the jails. Get into the refugee camps. Really make a nuisance of yourself . . . Look, if you like we could combine forces. Once we get off the collective farm circuit we'll find bags of good material for you. My name's Shorter, by the way. Owen Shorter. I'm doing it for one of the colour mags.
Mara (*emerging from her deepening melancholia*) One of the colour magazines?
Owen Don't say it in that tone of voice.

Mara One of the Sunday colour magazines?
Owen What's wrong with that?
Mara Oh my God.
Owen Oh, come on! I can't bear people who make snobbish remarks about the colour mags. They all read them. Look, I shall do a rather nice, rather well-written, rather up-market piece. Bit snide, perhaps. Bit fancy. Bit *wry*. Well, you read both of them, like everybody else. You know the kind of thing they go in for.
Mara I hope I know. I'm doing it for the other one.

Enter Ed. He is American—an able, cheerful, energetic, older man who speaks fluent Spanish. Like Owen, he is wearing an open-necked shirt. He rushes straight into the room and shakes hands with both of them as he talks

Ed *¡Lo siento! ¡Perdoname! ¡Me pegue a las sabanas! En casa no me llaman porque nunca duermo. Pero cuando llego aqui duermo de maravilla. ¡Es fantastico! ¡Me siento en casa aqui! ¡No se si es el aire, o el ambiente!*
Owen Yes, good, nice to meet you. (*Urgently*) Look, this is very embarrassing. It shouldn't have been allowed to happen, and I blame your press chap in London for not warning either of us . . .
Mara Does he speak English?
Owen Oh God . . . Do you speak English?
Mara Do—you—speak—English?
Ed Sure I speak English.
Owen Well, look, in our country we have a *competitive press*. This lady and I are working for newspapers which are *in competition* with each other.
Mara Capitalist press.
Owen I'm not defending it.
Mara Very bad.
Owen Terrible.
Mara Not like in your country.
Owen But it puts us in a very difficult position to find that we're writing about the same thing at the same time. It affects us as ordinary workers in the newspaper industry.

Ed grins

He doesn't understand.

Ed laughs

Mara He understands.

Ed My friends—don't worry! No, no—you're in Cuba now, and in Cuba all things are possible! We'll fix it somehow! We'll divide the country up between you. You take the east—you take the west. You take the sugar industry and art—you take coffee and literature. There's plenty going on here. You can each cut yourself a piece and come back for more. What do you want to see? What are you interested in?

Owen (*inhibited by Mara's presence*) Well . . .

Mara (*inhibited by Owen's presence*) Well . . .

Owen What I had in mind was a kind of . . .

Mara A sort of . . . overall . . .

Owen Rather general kind of . . .

Mara Impression.

Owen Yes, an impression. A general impression.

Mara What I was thinking of was more a kind of *personal* . . . well, yes . . . general impression.

Ed Two personal general impressions. O.K. Two personal general impressions coming up. Let's do it like this. (*To Mara*) You take the role of women in Cuban society. (*To Owen*) And you take the mechanization of agriculture.

Mara I don't want to do anything about women.

Owen I don't want to see a lot of collective farms.

Ed All right. (*To Mara*) How about the movie industry? Who are the new directors? Is the star system possible in the socialist cinema? (*To Owen*) For you—the weather.

Owen The weather?

Ed Do you realize what's happening here? The whole climate of the island is being changed! As soon as the current irrigation schemes are finished the Cuban people are going to have total control over their environment! How about that?

Mara I really just want to meet some . . . people.

Owen I think I'm more interested in the people angle.

Ed People? You'll meet people! You'll meet people like you've never met people before! Is this your first time here? I envy you, seeing it for the first time! Look, let me tell you something. There's one simple but vital fact about this country that you might as well get straight now, before you start: this is the greatest place on earth. Right? If you just keep that in mind you won't go far wrong . . . Where are they all? Out cutting cane? You wait here. I'll go find the *compañero*. We'll get it all set up for you. Regard this whole trip as a summer vacation.

Ed exits

Owen Oh God! Public relations men!
Mara He seems quite helpful.
Owen They're *all* helpful.
Mara He speaks good English, anyway.
Owen They *all* speak good English.
Mara Isn't he American?
Owen They're *all* American.
Mara What?
Owen As long as he gets us to opposite ends of the island. That's all I care about. You realize that people are going to be making jokes about this every time we set foot in the office?
Mara Set foot in which office?
Owen Yes, I suppose it's all right for you. You're not a professional. No-one expects professional standards. But I'm what they call a working journalist, and if I'm going to keep my job I have to maintain a minimum level of professional competence. I'm certainly not expected to come back from some highly expensive foreign assignment sharing my story with a horde of lady novelists. I'm not trying to be offensive. I only wish I had your talent. But there is a painful difference, often obscured by popular prejudice, between reporting something and making it up. Proper reporting involves getting quotes down accurately. Spelling names right. Checking. Then checking again. Boring, meticulous skills that you don't learn by writing fiction. It also involves coming face to face with the real world, a very muddled and overcrowded place where nothing has its name on it, and everything is somehow the wrong shape to be expressed in language. And if something is difficult to say, you've still got to say it. You can't just say something else instead, which I suppose you always can in a story. Even if it's a story as distinguished as *To Where I Lay*

Sighing. Dying. Sighing. God, it's as hot as a bowl of soup in here.

Ed returns with Angel. He is a Cuban in his mid-thirties, also in open neck and shirtsleeves—a sleepy man who chain-smokes and always has something wrong with him

Ed (*to Angel*) . . . *Acaso no entendimos el mensaje, pero hemos estado esperando aqui, en de quince* . . . (*To Owen and Mara*) Here he is. This is the man. Angel. Angel spelt "angel". An appropriate name, because he's going to be hovering over you like a guardian spirit for the next ten days. Angel, this is . . . (*To Mara*) I don't know your name . . .
Mara Hill.
Owen Mara Hill.
Ed Mara. Mara here wants you to arrange for her to meet some people. Maybe some people in the movie industry . . .

Angel nods sombrely, and makes a note

Mara (*anxiously*) No . . no . . .
Ed (*unperturbed*) Some people in the women's organizations . . .
Mara No . . no . .
Ed Some youth people—some trade union people . . .
Mara No . .
Ed Some of the old prostitutes . . . (*To Mara*) You know they have special places here where they rehabilitate the hookers? That could make a nice piece . . .
Mara No . . no . . .
Ed Take her to meet some of the hookers, all the same. And my friend here, whose name is . . .
Owen Owen.
Ed Owen . . . he wants to . . . What did you want to do, Owen?—he wants to see the irrigation schemes . . .

Angel continues to nod and note

Owen I do *not* want to see the irrigation schemes!
Ed (*to Owen*) They're changing the whole *climate*! It's the biggest story in the world, and no-one's got on to it yet!
Owen (*with ill-grace*) All right. All right. I'll look at the irrigation schemes.

Ed (*to Angel*) He'll take the irrigation schemes. And show him the ballet and the Central School of Art, too. But look after these people, Angel! They're friends of mine. And they represent very important British newspapers. Right?

Angel nods

Ed (*to Owen and Mara*) Right? Right? Right. Now, would you excuse us? Angel and I have to caucus a little to discuss *my* problems.

Owen Your problems? Why, do you want to go and look at the irrigation schemes?

Ed (*aside to Owen and Mara*) No, I want to try and meet one or two people like Sergio del Valle and Jose Abrantes in MININT. No use to you, because you don't speak the language. Come on, Angel, let's you and me go see the chief. (*To Owen and Mara*) He'll be right back to fix your schedules and arrange transportation for you. (*He shakes their hands*) So long. Glad to have met you. Hope I've been of some use. We may meet again some place in the island. People have a way of running into each other here. But don't forget, whatever you look at, this place just has to be the best there is. *¡Hasta la vista!*

Ed goes out

Angel (*to Owen and Mara*) I think you wait here, please. I think I come back.

Owen Just a moment. Who *was* that?

Angel That? That was Mr Budge.

Owen Mr Budge? And who's Mr Budge?

Angel I think he is friend of yours.

Owen We've never set eyes on him before. He must be a friend of *yours*.

Angel No. I think he come here yesterday from United States. I think he come here to write a book about this country for the University of Illinois.

Owen I see. Who are *you* doing it for? *Playboy* magazine?

Angel I think I am not writing about this country. I think I am only living here.

Angel goes out

Owen I think this heat is beginning to get me down.

The Lights go down on the foreground. Silhouetted against the sky, the Cast rearrange the chairs for the next scene, and remove the table and electric fan

Scene 2

The Lights go up on the foreground. The six chairs have been arranged in two rows of three to form the front and rear bench seats of a car. The back row is placed on a slightly higher level to make it visible

At the wheel sits Hilberto. He is middle-aged, black, shirt-sleeved, open-necked and is smoking a large cigar

Beside him, half-turned so as to be able to talk to the people in the back, sits Angel. On the back seat sit Owen and Mara, with Ed between them. Owen and Mara are both in low spirits; Ed as ebullient as ever.

Ed (*laughing*) But this is the great thing about Cuba! You never know what's going to happen next!
Owen There must be more than one Government car!
Ed Last time I was here everyone had a car!
Owen Everyone?
Ed All the visiting foreigners.
Owen They all had Cadillacs, like this?
Ed They all had Caddies.
Owen Power-operated windows?
Ed Power-operated windows. Chauffeur-driven.
Owen Chauffeur smoking a cigar?
Ed Big cigar. I could write an acceptable thesis on the fifties' Cadillac as the workhorse of the Revolution. Fine cars. All they needed was to be liberated and put at the disposal of the people.
Owen You and me.
Ed And Mara. (*He hugs her*)
Owen Then where are they now? Why have they taken them away from us again? Always the same story, isn't it? The Revolution comes, and we're all equal! We've all got chauffeur-

driven Cadillacs with power-operated windows! Then one day—what do you think?—the sign's been rewritten slightly: "Some foreign journalists are more equal than others." All of a sudden there are some of us who haven't got a chauffeur-driven Cadillac after all.

Ed Because they've been redistributed again! Woof!—like that! —they've been switched to the rural medical service. Or they're taking work-brigades out to the canefields. Or they're driving honeymoon couples around. In Cuba, my friend, things happen fast!

Angel When we arrive at the hotel I again make telephone call, is it possible we have also another car.

Ed Isn't it more fun like this, all riding along together? (*He hugs Mara*) *We're* having fun, anyway.

Angel Miss Hill is a very quiet person, I think.

Ed She's just sitting there and taking it all in.

Angel She is a very serious person.

Ed Yes, she's not missing anything.

Owen (*to Mara*) Are you all right? You look terrible.

Mara I'm just trying to think what I'm doing here.

Angel It is the heat, I think.

Ed It's the light. I remember the first time I came. It's the weight of the sky. She'll get used to it.

Owen Unless it's us.

Ed She'll get used to us, too. Seven days together in this car and we'll all be old friends.

Owen I've got perceptibly older in the last hour.

Ed Wait till we get to the sugar mill this afternoon!

Owen The sugar mill! I don't want to see a sugar mill!

Ed Owen, you're going to love the sugar mill.

Owen I've seen a sugar mill before.

Ed I've seen ten sugar mills before! So? Let's make it eleven! Owen, your life is not so full that you can't find room for one more sugar mill in it.

Owen I want to see the irrigation schemes! That's what I've come to Cuba for. I want to get away from *her*.

Ed (*to Mara*) Do *you* want to see the sugar mill?

Mara (*deeply depressed*) I don't care *what* I see.

Ed That's the girl! God, but I love this country! Look at that kid!

They all, except Hilberto, turn to look at what they are passing

Did you see? A boy walking along a country road. And the sun's shining. And there's no traffic on the road to hassle him.

Owen Apart from us.

Ed He's chewing a piece of sugar cane. And he's as happy as a mouse in a cracker-barrel! Look at this old feller.

They all turn to catch a glimpse of something else already disappearing behind them by the roadside

Sitting back on his donkey. Hand on hip. Straw hat on his head. Cigar in his mouth. Looking as if he owns the whole damned place. Which he does! That's Cuba back there, riding on that donkey!

Owen It may be Cuba, but I can't see how you can tell whether it's happy or not, when it's going past the windows at sixty miles an hour.

Ed Owen, you don't even have to look outside the car. This is Cuba, right here in front of you.

Owen What, Angel?

Ed No, not Angel. Angel's a diplomat. He speaks English, he travels. He's not a Cuban—he's one of us. He's just here to sell us Cuba. We don't take any notice of him.

Angel With a customer like Mr Budge, I think a salesman is not necessary.

Ed Don't worry, Angel—we'll split the commission. No, I mean Hilberto. I know these people, Owen. You look at Hilberto and you're looking at the real Cuba. You've got Cuba within touching distance. Right, Angel?

Angel He is one of the samples we send out with our representatives.

Ed You know what Hilberto was before the Revolution?

Owen A chauffeur.

Ed A chauffeur. You know what his employer was?

Owen A capitalist swine.

Ed Right, a businessman. A businessman who ran an import company. You know what they imported?

Owen Opium.

Ed Walking jiggers, from New York.

Owen What are walking jiggers?

Ed Liquor glasses that walk. You fill them with bourbon, you wind them up, and they get on their little feet and walk down to the other end of the bar. They're thought to cause amusing consternation among your alcoholic friends.

Owen A little amusing consternation is always welcome.

Ed Owen, this was in *Cuba*! The canecutters were all out of work from one sugar harvest to the next! Meanwhile, here was this comedian importing clockwork jiggers and Schmeckenbecker Schnitzel Banks. Do you know what a Schmeckenbecker Schnitzel Bank is?

Owen Some insult to the dignity of man.

Ed You put a nickel on top of it—the lid opens—and a hand comes out and grabs the nickel. That was Cuba, in nineteen fifty-nine. A Schmeckenbecker Schnitzel Bank. A hand that grabs money. *This* is Cuba today.

Owen This is the famous New Man they're trying to create here?

Ed This is a stage in the evolution of the New Man.

Owen I still can't see whether he's happy or not from the back of his neck.

Ed Let's ask him, then. *¿Como te va, amigo Hilberto?*

Hilberto *Estupendo.*

Ed He's stupendous.

Hilberto *Mi mujer está en la Habana y yo aqui. ¿Que mas querria un hombre?*

Ed laughs

Owen (*sourly*) Tell us, then.

Ed He says his wife's in Havana and he's here. What more can a man want?

Owen The New Man and the Old Jokes.

Ed This is the real Cuba you've got here, Owen. Earthy, open, good-humoured. Watch this man like a hawk. (*To Hilberto*) *Casi tienes tanta suerte que yo. Mi mujer esta en Urbana, Illinois.* (*To Mara, hugging her*) I said, he's almost as lucky as me. *My* wife's in Urbana, Illinois!

Owen (*gloomily*) *When* do we get to the sugar mill?

The Lights go down on the foreground. Once again the Cast are silhouetted as they rearrange the stage for the next scene. The sky fills with fleets of slow-moving burnished sub-tropical cumulus

Scene 3

The table has been brought back, with coffee-cups on it. Five of the chairs are arranged around the table

One of the places at the table is empty. In the others sit Angel, Hilberto, Mara, and Owen. Sub-tropical birds sing. It is very peaceful

Owen (*offering a box of cigars*) Mara? You can't write an article about Cuba if you haven't smoked a real Havana cigar.

Mara shakes her head

No? Oh, well, I have an exclusive on the cigars, anyway. Angel? If I'm pronouncing it right.

Angel No, I prefer cigarette. (*He takes a cigarette out of the breast pocket of his shirt*)

Owen Come on. Since I can buy these things in the bar for foreign currency, and you're on the ration.

Angel No, I must smoke cigarette. I have some trouble here, behind eyes.

Owen Hilberto?

Hilberto smiles, nods and takes one

Angel (*smiling*) I think you must not offer cigars to Hilberto. Always he takes one.

Hilberto (*to Angel*) *¿Podría tomar otro para mi amigo?*

Angel He asks is it possible he take another cigar. He has a friend who likes to smoke cigar.

Owen Sure.

Hilberto takes a second cigar, with a smiling acknowledgement, and tucks it in his shirt pocket

Angel Always he takes one. And always he takes another one.

Owen (*taking a cigar himself*) He looks like a man who's got a lot of friends.

Angel I think this is so. I think everywhere we shall go in Cuba, Hilberto shall have a friend.
Owen That's the way to do it, if you've got to travel all the time.

Hilberto lights Owen's cigar and his own

Gracias. I must say, one feels differently about a country after lunch. I can almost face the prospect of the sugar mill this afternoon. The mango-juice was bloody awful, if you want my frank opinion. But the steak wasn't bad, and this coffee's not bad, and the cigar's very good indeed. As, I might say, one would expect. You did ring the Ministry about getting another car?
Angel I telephone, but they did not know will it be possible. I must telephone once more tomorrow, I think.
Owen *Mañana y mañana y mañana* . . . Still, it's very peaceful sitting here with a large Havana cigar and a *buchito* of coffee in the heat of the day.

Hilberto finishes his coffee and stands up. He nods and smiles to the others, and goes out

Off to see his friend? Share out the spoils?
Angel (*smiling*) I think this is so.
Owen That's the way. Equal rations for all. Very peaceful . . . And that reminds me: where is our distinguished colleague?
Angel Sorry?
Owen Our American expert. (*To Mara*) Whose principal opus to date, incidentally, is a book entitled *Changing Concepts of Legality and Judicial Sanction in a Revolutionary Society*. As he shyly whispered to me in the Gents before lunch. (*At large*) He shot keenly out after the steak and never came back. I suppose he's somewhere out there in the midday sun stealing a march on us. Chatting up colourful local lawyers in idiomatic Spanish. (*To Mara*) Is he?
Mara I've no idea.
Owen Oh. I thought you might have.
Mara Why should *I* know where he is?
Owen I thought he might have confided in you.
Mara Why should he have confided in me?

Owen I thought you might be the sort of person that people put their arm round and confide in. Anyway, I expect he's out there in a canefield somewhere. Just the place for his researches into concepts of legality. I should think we're at least fifty miles from the nearest concept of legality, aren't we? Still, I suppose one might come down the road. In a Cadillac, probably.

Angel (*reproachfully*) Mr Budge speaks very well Spanish, I think.

Owen Yes. Mr Budge speaks very well Spanish.

Angel I think he understands very well Cuba.

Owen Sure. He understands very well Cuba. *If* that's an advantage. Well, there are two different techniques in journalism, aren't there. There's Mr Budge's technique. You speak the language, you have inside contacts, you know everything there is to know. And what happens? Your inside contacts tell you everything in confidence, so you can't use it, and you never notice anything else because you know it all already. Then there's the technique which Mara and I favour. We don't speak the language. We don't know anything. We don't know anyone. We just let it all flow in upon us. Don't we, Mara? We're not ashamed to ask naïve questions. (*Very casually*) Oh, and that reminds me. As we were driving along back there through the great empty spaces, if you remember, we were chatting about the famous work camps you have here.

Angel Work camps, yes.

Owen We were interrupted by another enthusiastic shout from our well-informed American colleague. Just as I was about to ask something.

Mara I still don't understand why you think he should have confided in me.

Owen (*to Mara*) A joke. A light-hearted remark in passing. (*To Angel*) Yes, I was saying, if you remember, what a sensible and humane way it was to deal with anti-social elements, putting them in labour camps——

Angel Work camps.

Owen (*quickly*) Work camps. (*Casually*) What I was wondering was if a case had to be . . . trailed all through the courts before someone could be sent to the camps, or whether the police could just decide for themselves, informally, without any fuss.

Angel (*cautiously*) If people can be convicted without trial?

Owen Yes. To save time and expense, and so on. Change your mind, by the way. Have a cigar.

Owen offers the cigars. Angel hesitates, his hand raised to take a cigar, thinking

Mara Can you get an abortion here?

Owen bangs the box of cigars down on the table in fury

Angel (*distracted*) If is possible to have abortion?

Owen Do you need one this instant? Or could it, without too much risk, wait until Angel and I have finished our conversation?

Mara I'm sorry. I thought I heard you say something about labour wards.

Owen Labour camps.

Angel Work camps.

Owen Work camps.

Mara Oh. Sorry.

Owen (*offering Angel the cigars again*) Angel, I think you were just about to take a cigar, and tell me about ways of speeding up the administration of justice.

Angel (*his hand hesitates over the cigars again while he thinks—then he forgets about them*) But I think the question if is possible to have abortion is very interesting. To understand this we must first consider what was the situation here before the Revolution . . .

Ed enters

Owen Ed! Come and rescue us! Miss Hill and Angel are having a gynaecological conversation.

Ed Look at it! Look at it out there! Green canefields. Blue sugarloaf mountains. And royal palms everywhere like some kind of standing firework display. Look at them, rocketing sixty feet up into the air, then exploding in green. And those clouds. They often build up in the afternoon like that. Come packing in on the Trades. Towered cities of cumulus and strato-cumulus. That's Cuba up there. Shining. Changing. Another world. Floating free of money and greed.

Owen They haven't got rid of money yet.

Ed They will. They are. That's how it's all going to be one of these days.

Owen Strato-cumulus and Hilberto-nimbus.

Ed You wait. Hey, I met the most fantastic character, while you good people were sitting over your coffee and liqueurs. I met the most unbelievable personage, Owen, while you were enjoying your postprandial cigar.

Owen Go on.

Ed I went into the kitchens—Rule One in life: Get out of the dining-room and into the kitchens—and there in the kitchens was this little man repairing the Frigidaire. So we got talking, and it turns out that before the Revolution he was the biggest independent distributor of blue movies on the island. Now he mends ice-boxes! Goes to cut cane every weekend with the rest of the workshop. And loves every minute of it! Never been so happy in his life! But the stories he told me about the old days in the blue movie business! He had the whole kitchen cracking up!

Angel I think this man's story is quite significant. I think there are many people here who have such a history to tell.

Owen I met rather a character, too. Strange as it may seem. Have you noticed the old waiter? The one with the shakes?

Ed The one who speaks English?

Owen Sure, the one who speaks English. That doesn't make him any less genuine, speaking English. Plenty of people here spoke English in the old days.

Ed Of course. Because this was virtually an American colony, and they had to speak the language of the imperial power . . .

Owen Right, right, right. Anyway, he cornered me in the Gents. Held me with his skinny hand and glittering eye while he told me how he visits his son in the States every summer. He said he likes to get the ten o'clock plane from Havana to Miami, so he has plenty of time to catch the midday train from Miami to Baltimore. How about that?

Ed (*tactfully*) Owen, there aren't any planes from Havana to Miami. There's been no public air service between Cuba and the States for over ten years.

Angel I think Mr Budge is correct in this particular.

Owen That's the *point*! That's what's so pathetic about it. Here's this old man, and he's still living in nineteen fifty-nine.

Ed Oh, I see. Well, he grabbed hold of me and gave me all that stuff, too.
Owen Oh.
Mara He told me, as well.
Owen Oh dear. Not in the Gents. I trust?
Mara In the bar.
Owen It was more colourful in the Gents. (*To Ed*) Did he tell you in the Gents?
Ed He told me in Spanish.
Owen Of course.
Ed And in Spanish he said it all in the past tense. That's all that's pathetic about him—he can only conjugate English verbs in the present.
Owen I'll tell you the only thing that demonstrates.
Ed What?
Angel How much Mr Budge misses by speaking the language.
Owen Thank you.
Mara I met a woman in the Ladies who'd just murdered her lover.

Owen and Ed both turn to look at her, impressed

She was pregnant by him. She found him in the cane with another woman. She picked up a cane-cutter's machete and hacked him to death. They took her before a People's Court. The judges were three women. They fined her twenty pesos for damaging the machete.

Owen and Ed stare at her for a moment. Then each quietly slips out a notebook and pencil to note it down

Owen (*hesitating*) Just a moment. In English she said all this?
Mara In Spanish.
Owen You don't know any Spanish.
Mara I don't know the words, but I can understand the sense.

Hilberto enters. He is still smoking his cigar, but the second cigar in his shirt pocket has gone, and he is carrying, as inconspicuously as possible, something that hangs down from his hand and is loosely wrapped in crumpled newspaper

Owen What about you, Hilberto? Have you met any colourful characters hanging about the local public conveniences? Did you find your friend? *¿Amigo?*

Hilberto (*embarrassed, trying to cross with his parcel concealed behind him*) *Si, si. Amigo . . .*

Owen Yes, I see you did. The cigar's gone. (*He gestures to his own shirt pocket*)

Hilberto (*putting his hand to his shirt pocket*) *Cigarro. Si, si . . .*

Owen I hope he was grateful. Has he given you something, then? What is it? Yesterday's newspaper?

Hilberto half-shows the bundle. It quacks loudly. Smiling, slightly abashed, he hustles it away

The Lights on the foreground go down. The sky becomes completely black as the foreground Lights fade up for the next scene

SCENE 4

Four separate pools of light, widely separated on different parts of the set. In the two outer areas of light sit Ed and Owen, in the two inner areas Angel and Mara. Each of them is using a raised level of the stage as a seat, and a chair as a desk. Owen, Ed and Angel each have a portable typewriter balanced on their chairs. Mara has a pad of paper, and is chewing on a fountain-pen. All four are thinking. Owen wipes his face

The sound of cicadas

Owen, Ed and Angel all begin to type. Mara continues to chew her pen, gazing gloomily into space

The typing stops. All three typists think. Owen and Ed wipe the sweat from inside the neck of their shirts.

Owen winds the paper (plus carbon and copy) out of his machine and reads what he has written.

Owen Wednesday PM. Eighty-five in the shade. Drive for one and a half hours. Swerve to avoid chicken—kill goose. Arrive sugar mill. Sugar mill v. impressive. Examine it minutely, and definitely establish that it is indeed a sugar mill. It mills sugar. No deception here. Another two hours drive to Government rest-house. See a mirage of iced rum daiquiris floating over road ahead of car. Our friend from Urbana, Illinois, however, spots cane-cutting brigade at work in the fields. Proposes stopping and joining them.

He stops to make a correction to his text by hand. Ed rips off his shirt, wipes his chest with it, and throws it aside. He flexes his arms and massages his shoulder muscles

Insists, against the united opposition of the rest of the world's press, on stopping and joining them. Plunges in with many a joyous liberated cry in the local dialect, many a hearty clap on back for new-found comrades, many a dislocating squeeze for horny cane-cutting hands. Borrows brigade-leader's machete and sets to work. Everyone, naturally, stops work to watch this laughing demonstration of international solidarity. Our Comrade from the Ministry, meanwhile, who never moves hand or foot unless the demands of revolutionary duty are overwhelming, watches with an encouraging smile.

He stops and thinks about this. Angel, who is also checking through what he has typed, absent-mindedly takes a cigarette from the pack in his breast pocket and lights it. Owen alters his text

. . . who never moves hand or foot . . . and who has developed a special slow labour-saving way of walking, and a special slow labour-saving way of sitting in a chair, and a special slow labour-saving way of smoking a cigarette, watches with an encouraging smile. Would join in himself, he says, but unfortunately has pain behind the eyes brought on by smoking too much. (*He stops, and adds another sentence*) Unless it's by sitting up late writing solemn reports on us all for the Ministry.

Angel suddenly dissolves in laughter at what he is reading

Hilberto—our admirable chauffeur, who already seems to have given up the use of money, there being nothing in the shops to buy, and who devotes his spare hours instead to the noble and uplifting practice of barter—Hilberto gets out of the car, utters some long-drawn cry indicative of revolutionary enthusiasm, and sits down in the shade. In the end even our distinguished but apparently catatonic lady novelist manages to get out of the car. No doubt all her lady novelist's instincts are aroused by the sensuous interplay of swaying cane and glittering steel. Or just possibly by the no less sensuous interplay of rippling Illinois muscle and flashing Illinois teeth . . .

Owen winds more paper into his machine. Ed types a few more words, then winds the paper up in the machine to read it

Ed In the end even Owen is shamed into borrowing a machete and pitching in. Makes heroic but ineffectual effort to cut cane while continuing to look down nose. Takes half-a-dozen swipes, accompanying each one with a strange little grunt, possibly inspired by old recordings of Leadbelly singing "Take This Hammer". Then stops. Announces: "This bloody bill-hook's blunt. That's the bloody trouble. In England a good hedger always keeps his bloody blade absolutely like a bloody razor." Whereupon he demonstrates to the ignorant natives how blunt the machete is by running his thumb along it . . .

Owen begins to type, but stops at once to examine his bandaged thumb. Ed thinks of an improvement

. . . by running his bloody thumb along it.

He types this, and continues to type. Owen turns his head to listen, then prepares to type himself

Owen Now the noise of his typewriter comes through the thin walls of the resthouse like relentless machine-gun fire, as he hammers down the telling statistics, the colourful quotes.

Owen types. Ed stops, and reads through what he has written

Ed Now the night air is heavy with the heavy irony of his type-writer reporting on the day's events. Good God, it stammers, no eggs and bacon for breakfast. Not a single gold swizzle-stick for sale in the shops. Just a frightful embarrassing cheer-fulness and enthusiasm everywhere. And this frightful embar-rassing American who actually seems to like it here . . . What should we do without Owen? I love him. I just worry a little that he may be driving poor Mara crazy . . .

Ed starts typing again. Mara looks desperately from Owen to Ed, throws down her pen, and covers her ears. Owen stops typing, and reads through

Owen The noise must be drowning the faint scritch-scratch of the distinguished lady novelist's pen, as she scribbles down her steaming lady novelist's thoughts . . .

He listens. Ed also stops and listens. Mara slowly sinks down in despair, until her head is resting on the paper in front of her

(*Typing*) Now it's stopped. Now nothing but the cicadas and the night.

Owen winds the paper out of the typewriter and picks up a pen to check it through. Then he stops to listen. So do Ed and Angel

Hilberto is picking his way on, carefully tiptoeing through the darkness between the four areas of light

Owen adds to his typescript by pen

And the sound of someone tiptoeing along the corridor.

Owen listens. Ed and Angel listen. The click of a light-switch; and Hilberto is standing in a fifth pool of light. This area, too, has a chair in it. Owen writes

The click of a light being switched off. Miss Hill's light? Mr Budge's? Do I detect the soft touch of romance in the rest-house?

Owen strains his ears. Hilberto quietly sits down on the edge of a raised level. He reaches into his shirt and takes out something wrapped in newspaper. Still being careful not to make a noise he unwraps not the real duck that quacked earlier, but a pull-along toy duck. He puts it on the floor and pulls it along

Toy Duck Quack quack quack quack.

Hilberto hushes it guiltily. Black-out

The sky lightens to silhouette the Cast as they rearrange the scene, then brightens to the full, hard, daytime blue

Scene 5

When the Lights come up on the foreground they reveal the table with breakfast things on it and five of the chairs around it

Angel and Hilberto are sitting at the table. They have finished breakfast. Hilberto is smoking a cigar. Angel gets out a cigarette and lights it with his usual minimal movements

Owen enters, holding an unsealed envelope

Angel Good morning.
Owen Good morning. *Buenos dias*, Hilberto. (*He sits*)
Hilberto *Buenos.*
Angel And how are you this morning?
Owen I have a stomach-ache and diarrhoea. That's how I am. How are you?
Angel I have pain behind eyes. I think this is because I smoke too much.
Owen I expect so. *¿Como estás*, Hilberto?

Hilberto shrugs

Angel He has pain in head.
Owen That's because he smokes too much.
Angel I think this is so. Did you sleep well?
Owen No. Did you sleep well?
Angel No.
Owen (*looks unenthusiastically at the glass in front of him*) Orange-juice. That's about all I can manage this morning. (*He drinks, then stops, and carefully puts the glass back on the table*) Mango-juice.
Angel I am sorry to say that this morning there is no orange-juice.
Owen I am impressed, I must admit. I am reluctantly impressed. To produce a shortage of orange-juice in a sub-tropical island one hundred and fifty miles off the coast of Florida is a striking tribute to the power of economic planning. Coffee—that's one of the principal crops of the island. Or was. Do you think a last cupful survives anywhere?
Angel I'm sorry?
Owen *Coffee.*
Angel You'd like some coffee?
Owen I'd like some coffee.
Angel I ask. (*He looks round*)
Owen (*taking the typescript out of the envelope and writing on it*) "Thursday AM, breakfast. Stomach-ache. Diarrhoea. No orange-juice. Exclamation mark." I always keep a diary when I'm away on jobs. Send a carbon off to my wife each morning. The children take turns to read it out over breakfast. Keeps

them in touch. (*He puts the letter back in the envelope and seals it*) Where's Batman this morning?

Angel I'm sorry?

Owen The Hero of Socialist Labour. The Stakhanovite from Urbana, Illinois.

Angel Oh, Mr Budge. He finish breakfast before we come.

Owen That's bad news. He'll have cleared half Cuba of sugar cane by now. Before lunchtime you're going to have all the *macheteros* unemployed again.

Angel The English have a proverb, I think, which says: "It's the early bird that gets the worm!"

Owen You've got it round the wrong way. "It's the early worm that gets the bird."

Angel I'm sorry?

Owen And talking about the bird, where is she?

Angel I'm sorry?

Owen Our distinguished lady novelist. The early worm hasn't got her already, has he? He got off to a rapid start yesterday. I don't know whether you noticed. Little cuddles in the back of the car. Little pats on the arm.

Angel Oh. You think Mr Budge is enamoured of Miss Hill? (*Laughs*) Well! Perhaps this is so!

Owen I'll bet you a box of cigars that they're away before we get back to Havana. No, I'll go further. I'll bet you a glass of orange-juice.

Enter Mara, wearing dark glasses

Good morning, my dear. We were just talking about you.

Angel Good morning.

Mara sits down, with a scarcely perceptible nod at the company

Owen How are you feeling this morning?

Mara shakes her head

That's how we're feeling, too. He has a pain behind the eyes. *He* has a pain in the head. I have a stomach-ache and diarrhoea. What I hate most is the lethargy. I can't imagine how I shall ever find the energy to stop sitting here making patronising jokes that Angel can't understand. Let alone walk all the way outside to the car. Did you sleep well?

Mara No.

Owen Nor did we. My mosquito netting didn't seem to let air through.

Angel The only thing that my mosquito netting let through was mosquitoes.

Owen Let me make the jokes, Angel. I'm iller than you are. Anyway, cheer up, my dear. We've only got about three hundred miles to do this morning. Haven't we, Angel? Then we'll get to the new town. Is it the new town today?

Angel Today, yes, we go to the new town.

Owen You see? You always get to a new town somewhere around the second day. Or more probably to a large area of hot dust where the new town will one day be. Come on, my dear—drink up your lovely juice. It'll put roses in your cheeks.

Mara sips reluctantly at her glass of juice, then stops in disgust

It's lovely mango-juice. The orange-juice wells have dried up. God, I feel terrible! (*To Angel*) Where can I post this?

Angel (*taking the letter*) I think I can do this.

Owen How long does air mail to England take?

Angel I think five weeks.

Owen Five weeks? Air mail?

Angel Sometimes. Sometimes less quick.

Owen But a pigeon could fly it faster than that! What are they using—carrier gnats?

Mara is suddenly shaken by sobs

I beg your pardon?

Angel She weeps, I think.

Owen What is it?

Angel Please tell us what is the matter.

Mara shakes her head and sobs. The others look at each other. Hilberto tilts his head to mean: "but that's the kind of thing that happens"

Owen Has something upset you? Something we've said? Something that happened?

Angel You have pain?

Hilberto (*gesturing in turn at his head, stomach, and throat*) *Jaqeca. L'estomaco. O puede ser la garganta.*

Owen (*to Angel*) What were we talking about?
Angel The air mail.
Owen Is it the postal service that's worrying you? Look, we can't do anything unless you tell us what the matter is.
Mara It's the mornings here.
Owen The mornings?
Angel (*to Owen*) What?
Owen It's the mornings.

Hilberto looks at Angel interrogatively

Angel *Las mañanas.*
Mara Once we've got to lunchtime I can stand it. It's when you can see the whole day stretching ahead of you, and you know you can't get to the next day until you've got all the way through this one . . .
Angel (*to Owen*) What?
Owen She's . . . a little depressed. Long day ahead. Feel better with some lunch inside her.
Angel (*to Mara*) I think then you must eat some breakfast. Shall I ask, is there some beef or some pork?
Mara Excuse me.

Mara rushes blindly out

Silence. Angel catches Owen's eye, and gives a little sympathetic smile and shrug

Owen I'm sorry about this.
Angel *I* am sorry.
Owen Terrible, seeing one's fellow-countrymen behaving embarrassingly abroad.
Angel Everyone sometimes must be sad. Everyone sometimes must weep.
Owen Do you think there's a Cuban delegation bursting into tears at this very moment in some heart-breaking grim hotel in the suburbs of Birmingham? No mango-juice on the breakfast menu. A new town and a cocoa works looming over the day. Stomachs in dull rebellion. Blinding sunshine boiling their brains.
Angel (*politely*) Perhaps.
Owen Or perhaps not.

Angel I think I must go and look is she OK.
Owen I think you'd better. Cuba's going to be getting a terrible press if she goes home in this mood.

Angel exits

I suppose I ought to go, too. Fellow-countryman in distress. Fellow-countrywoman. But how typical of that lot to send out some manic-depressive amateur! Oh God oh God oh God oh God.

Hilberto lifts his head interrogatively, not understanding

Oh Dios oh Dios oh Dios oh Dios.
Hilberto (*matter-of-factly*) *Oh, si.*

Owen exits

Hilberto helps himself to the two unfinished glasses of mango-juice

Mara enters, in low spirits but no longer crying. She sits in her former place

Silence

Mara The children have gone to France for the week, to stay with their father. The cats are with some people across the street. Mrs Sparrow, who lives downstairs—she's in hospital with her hip. The house is empty. It's the house I keep thinking about, not the children. The table I work at. It's got two old pennies under the leg to stop it rocking. There's a stone Dundee marmalade jar I keep pencils and biros in. That's what I look at while I think. "James Keiller and Son Ltd. Dundee and Croydon." I work in the kitchen—there isn't anywhere else. You can hear the women shouting at their children in the flats opposite. And the traffic. It never stops. I like the traffic—I never realized before. You know there are people out there. Working. Moving about. Living other lives. Every now and then the glass in the window starts to purr. That's a train on the Northern Line. Sometimes, on fine mornings, the sun catches the windows of a bus, and a flash of light runs through the room like quicksilver. There's an old sofa under the window, with books and coffee-cups and piles of dead newspapers on it. That's where the phone usually ends up, on top of the papers. Every time it rings I think, "Now things are going to be all right". Perhaps it's ringing now. Perhaps a bus is going by. Well, that's all me—the phone, the bus, the walls, the table. There's nothing left of me here without it. Just the bare quick.

Silence. Hilberto carefully puts down his cigar. He takes out a coin, shows it to Mara, and makes it disappear. He repeats the trick, to show her how it is done. Then he gets down on his knees, slowly lowers his head till it is on the floor, and stands on his head. Mara watches him gravely

Owen enters. He stares at them

Hilberto gets back on his feet, and bows

Thank you.

Hilberto indicates the expression on Owen's face. Mara smiles

Hilberto (*indicating Mara to Owen, triumphantly*) Aaaaaaah!

The foreground Lights go down. The sky fills with cumulus, and the sound of a cha-cha-cha is heard

Scene 6

Car and sky

Hilberto is driving. Angel is asleep beside him. Ed is in the middle of the back seat, with Owen and Mara on either side of him. All three are asleep. Mara's head is resting on Ed's shoulder

The cha-cha-cha continues, quiet and soothing

Hilberto swings the wheel, and the sleepers all keel over as the car makes a right-angle turn. Owen's head sinks on to Ed's free shoulder. Heads rock and jiggle as the car crosses rough ground. Owen's head works its way down Ed's chest into his lap

The movement stops. Hilberto applies the handbrake, and switches off the engine and radio. The music ceases. Then he settles down in his seat to sleep himself

Silence

Angel (*slowly, blearily waking and looking out*) Ladies and gentlemen, I think we have arrived.

Pause

Owen (*getting himself out of Ed's lap, and looking out*) New town?

Angel New town.

Owen groans, closes his eyes, and settles his head back on Ed's shoulder

Angel (*getting out of the car*) I go and look is anyone here.

Angel goes off

Ed (*waking and stretching hugely*) New town?
Owen (*with his eyes still closed*) New town.
Ed Woof! That was some sleep! I feel like I'm the New Man already. The New Man for the New Town. Right! Let's go!

Ed extracts himself from Owen and Mara, and gets out of the car. He stands gazing up at the clouds and flexing his muscles. Owen, unsupported, heels over until he hits the seat. He wakes up sharply

Owen What? Oh, I thought the bed had collapsed. *Now* what's he up to? He's not going to start laying bricks and mixing cement, is he? Some people don't understand—reporters are supposed to say what the world's like, not make the world like they say. (*To Mara*) We're here, love. Don't you want to see the new town?
Mara (*opening her eyes and looking out briefly*) I think I'll stay in the car.
Owen That's how it looks to me, too. I should sit outside, though. It'll be like a can of beans cooking in here.

No response

How are you feeling now? Any better?

Mara shakes her head minimally, her eyes closed

No, nor am I. I feel as if I've collapsed inwards, like an old brown cardboard box. I must say, I could quite happily burst into tears myself. Well, you stay here and rest, then. If there's anything in this place I'll fill you in afterwards.

He pats her arm sympathetically, and gets out of the car

Ed Fantastic. I mean literally. What did Prospero call it on his island? The cloud-capped towers of a vision.
Owen The baseless fabric of a vision.
Ed All right, then. But the cloud-capped towers, the gorgeous palaces . . .
Owen Shall dissolve. Leave not a rack behind.
Ed But didn't he go on to say, we are such stuff as dreams are made on?
Owen Dust, so far as I can see. Old paper bags. Rusty scaffolding.
Ed They'll build it fast enough, don't you worry. This is the downtown centre we're standing on.
Owen You've been here before?
Ed I've been here. I've seen the plans. I've talked to the planners. I tell you, Owen, I know this town as well as I know the town I was born in. Two years from now there's going to be fountains splashing here, and bands playing under the trees.
Owen Children howling for ice-cream.
Ed Boys meeting their dates under the clock.
Owen Old men with nowhere else to go.
Ed I can see it, Owen.
Owen Sharp eyes, Ed.
Ed Twenty twenty.
Owen Twenty-one twenty-one.
Ed When *you* look you see only dust and scaffolding?
Owen Holes for windows. Holes for drains. Holes.
Ed Let me tell you something, Owen. Those holes no longer exist. That dust is no longer there.
Owen I'm imagining it all?
Ed No, that's the trouble. If you were imagining it there'd be no problem. But you're seeing it.
Owen Go on.
Ed Light from that pile of scaffolding is reaching you right now.
Owen So it seems to me.
Ed But that light left the pile of scaffolding some while back.

Owen Some very short while back, Ed.
Ed Very short.
Owen Micro-seconds.
Ed A fraction of a micro-second. But even so, not now. In the past. In the past as surely as the light that left Andromeda two million years ago.
Owen Oh, come on!
Ed Owen, what's past is past!
Owen Not if it's only this instant past!
Ed This instant past is as past as slightly pregnant is pregnant! That pile of scaffolding is gone. You can't go back to it. It's over and done with. Lost. Closed off. As inaccessible as Andromeda. The present is history, Owen. Something we can no longer affect. Something that no longer affects us. The present is not where we live. Where we live—where we really live, where we breathe, where we act, where we feel—is the future. What do you look at when you drive a car? The car? No—you look at the road ahead. You live not where you are now but where you expect to be. You live in the world that can still be affected by your decisions and shaped by your actions. You live in the world that can still up and kill you. And that world is the world of things that are still coming into existence—of things that might be and things that might be made to be. The future, Owen! That's what's real! That's what's accessible to us! That's the only home we have! And what you're looking at here, Owen, is not dust and emptiness, but ten thousand people and their lives. And the lives of their children. And of their children's children. Ten million people through ten million years.

Pause

Owen I'd like to live in that marble palace.
Ed You can see a marble palace? Well, maybe you can, too.
Owen (*looking upwards*) A soft white marble palace with soft white marble domes and towers. It's turning into an apricot nylon cathedral even as we look at it.

Angel enters

Poor Angel. You're soaking wet.

Angel Wet? I? No?
Owen That's funny. You're standing in the middle of the fountains.
Angel Sorry?
Owen You want us to start work.
Angel The Chairman of the Regional Committee of Planning waits to show us round. I think. I think we must go in this way.
Ed Lead on.
Angel Where is Miss Hill?
Owen Miss Hill is lying in the car, feeling like an old brown cardboard box.

Angel crosses to the car and looks at Mara

Ed (*to Owen*) But, seriously, for an awful lot of people at present living in bug-ridden palm-leaf cabins, what this town is going to be in two years' time is truly much more important and much more real than what it is now.
Owen And of course you're absolutely right. As always. Let me just ask you something. While the opposition is alas incapacitated. What percentage of the labour force on a site like this would be supplied by the local labour camps?
Ed Work camps.
Owen Work camps . . .

Ed and Owen go off

Hilberto is still asleep in the front seat, Mara in the back seat. Angel goes on gazing at her. She opens her eyes, then closes them again

Mara Tell me something.
Angel Yes?
Mara About yourself.
Angel What do you wish to know?
Mara Anything. (*She opens her eyes*) I know more about the sugar industry than I do about you.
Angel About me I think there is nothing to be said.
Mara Tell me about your childhood.
Angel Oh . . . (*He shrugs*)

Mara What were your parents like? Did you get on with them? Were you happy? Did you have any sisters or brothers? Were you poor? Did you chew sugar cane?

He sits down and thinks

Angel My father he worked in a factory.
Mara He was a worker, an ordinary worker?
Angel (*suddenly laughing*) A worker? My father? I think he gives a cry of pain in his grave when he hears you say this. Many things my father thought he was. Businessman, musician, philosopher. But ordinary worker—I think this idea never came into his head.
Mara What did he do in the factory?
Angel Mostly, I think, he laughed.
Mara Laughed? He was so happy in his work?
Angel I think yes, he was possibly happy.
Mara Someone happy. How fine!
Angel Perhaps. It depends upon what things make you happy.
Mara What things made your father happy?
Angel In this factory where he worked they made shoes. But my father did not make shoes. My father made wages. He counted the money, and put it in small envelopes. The other men they stood in workshops and they touched wax and thread and the skins of animals; my father he sat in an office and he touched nothing but coins and banknotes. So of course he felt himself to be a different sort of person. He felt himself to be more like the businessman who owned the factory. Because shoes are only shoes, but money is money; and in money you can see the possibility of many things. You hold money in your hand and you hold a thing that can turn by magic into a cigar, or into a bottle of rum, or into a woman. Or even into a pair of shoes. Or even perhaps, if you have very good luck, into more money. Every day my father comes home and he tells my mother and my brothers and me about the men. The men are the other men, the ones who make the shoes. "These people!" he says. "These people!" And he laughs. He laughs because always these people want things they cannot afford. They like to get married. They like to have children. They like to eat. And my father, who puts the money in the envelopes each week, knows that there is not enough to pay for all these

big ideas. So he shakes his head and he laughs and he laughs. "These people!" he says. And this is what makes him happy.

Mara Your father sounds like Mr Shorter.

Angel I think that Mr Shorter does not like many things in Cuba.

Mara Mr Shorter looks at everything and sees nothing.

Angel I think he looks even at you and sees nothing. I think when he looks at you and sees nothing, you look at yourself and see nothing also.

Mara You have eyes like barley sugars. Did anyone ever tell you that before?

Angel I think no-one did tell me that before. Barley . . .?

Mara Sugars. Sweets.

Angel You are feeling better.

Mara Yes. That's what I needed all the time. Barley sugar.

The Lights go down on the foreground

Scene 7

Car and sky, as in the previous scene

But Mara, Hilberto and Angel have disappeared. Owen is now lying on the ground by the car

Ed wearily enters

Ed There you are.

Owen Here I am.

Ed How long have you been back?

Owen One hour and seventeen minutes.

Ed (*sitting*) Woof! Hot.

Owen It seems so to me.

Ed Dusty.

Owen Aren't we living in the past?

Ed Gets everywhere. Down your throat.

Owen Think of the future.

Ed I am thinking of the future. I'm thinking of beer.

Owen Beer? Where will the beer be? In the fountains? Drifting in a fine cloud of spray across the Park of Culture and Rest?

Ed In our hotel, Owen.

Owen In the fountains, I believe it. In the hotel, no.

Ed Of course they'll have beer. What are we waiting for? Where's Angel?

Owen They've run out of Angel.

Ed Where's Hilberto?

Owen The supply of Hilberto has been disrupted by counter-revolutionaries.

Ed Even Mara seems to have disappeared. What's wrong with her? Is she depressed about something?

Owen I thought she might have confided in you.

Ed Why should she confide in me?

Owen I thought you were establishing something of a bridge-head there.

Ed I shouldn't say that.

Owen It looked like a bridgehead to me. Beaches cleared. Tanks ashore.

Ed No, no. I mean, I think she's very sweet.

Owen Sweet? Like sugar? What an extraordinary use of language.

Ed Also I feel sorry for her. You put her down all the time.

Owen I put her down? Ed, I've been scrupulously polite and friendly to her! I told her I'd fill in for her while she's ill. I've told her how to cope with guided tours and Government press officers. What do you want me to do? Write the piece for her? Good God, we're supposed to be stamping on each other's toes to get the story! No, as a matter of fact *I* feel sorry for her. Pitched into this kind of job without any preparation. It takes a long time to learn this trade, and the only way to do it is to start right in at the beginning on a local newspaper, covering funerals.

Ed I've never covered a funeral.

Owen You're in a different trade. But you wrote *Changing Concepts of whatever it was in a Revolutionary doodah.* I should think that's much the same sort of thing.

Ed Oh. Thanks.

Owen No. I mean it's *factual.* It involves standing at the gate of the cemetery getting the names of the mourners. Poor bloody Mara. I think she is actually cracking up.

Ed Owen, she'll get over it.

Owen You know she burst into tears at breakfast this morning?

Ed I've seen plenty of healthy, happy people burst into tears at breakfast.

Owen Well, I think we're going to see it build up. I think in a few days time she's going to be bursting into tears at lunch, tea and dinner as well.

Ed What? Just because she never reported funerals?

Owen She's probably got personal problems, too, hasn't she? Poor lass. I expect that's why she took the trip on. Desperate attempt to get away from some boyfriend, or some writer's block. No, I'm very sympathetic, believe me. It's just that I have a horrible suspicion, like a cold coming on at the back of the throat, that I'm going to end up escorting her back to London under sedation.

Ed Owen, what has that woman done to you?

Owen You look at this dustheap and you see a new town with fountains playing. You look at Mara and you don't see her sobbing quietly all the way from Havana to Madrid and from Madrid to Heathrow? With me beside her trying to stop her disturbing the other passengers? And her going to the toilet, all dazed and unsteady, and falling into people's laps?

Ed You've really been thinking about this, haven't you?

Owen Here they come. Take a good look at her. Tell me what *you* think.

Mara, Angel and Hilberto enter. Angel is carrying Mara's shoes. They all have wet hair; Mara is combing hers out. They are dancing a cha-cha-cha

Ed (*seriously*) Hi, Mara . . . How are things?

Mara bursts out laughing. Angel and Hilberto smile

You seem a little brighter.

Mara It's the sight of you two. Sitting there in little heaps like that. We can't think what you remind us of. Angel says two candle-stubs just before they finally go out. I think two rather moth-eaten old cock-sparrows who've been taking a dust-bath.

Ed Miraculous cure. Where have you been?

Angel We have been swimming.
Owen *Swimming?*
Ed In the fountains. What did I tell you?
Mara There's a river just the other side of the road.
Ed And I never thought to bring a swimsuit with me!
Mara What do you need a swimsuit for?
Angel On the invitation is written "Dress informal"!
Mara You should have come.
Owen Some of us happened to be looking at the new town.
Mara Was that fun?
Owen Was it fun? Of course it wasn't fun. It merely happens to be what we came here for.
Mara Anyway, we all feel a million times better. Don't we, Angel!
Angel I feel well, I think.
Mara Angel feels well. Hilberto feels well. I feel well.
Ed (*to Owen*) I told you—in Cuba anything can happen.

Hilberto exits

Owen (*to Ed*) If this is the mania, I preferred the depression.
Angel (*ushering them towards the car*) I think we must go now to our hotel. There we shall find very tall glasses with rum and crushed ice in them.
Ed Long cool drinks! I'll murder them!

Ed gets into the back of the car. Owen stands aside to let Mara get into the back as well, but instead she gets into the front, and sits in the middle. Angel gets in beside her. He takes the comb and combs his hair. Owen gets into the back beside Ed

Hilberto enters, carrying a used shovel

A shovel? There may be snowdrifts?
Angel (*grinning*) This shovel is a present. Hilberto has also here a friend.
Mara To think that he started out in life with nothing but a spare cigar.
Ed At this rate he'll end up as President of General Motors.

Hilberto grins, realizing that remarks are being passed. He puts the shovel under the feet of the people in front, and gets in behind the wheel. He borrows the comb from Angel and combs his hair

Mara Oh! I feel . . . *alive!* (*She kisses Hilberto on the cheek*)
Hilberto (*cheerfully*) Whee—heeeeeee!

Mara kisses Angel on the cheek

Angel That's nice!
Ed A long cool kiss.
Hilberto Whee—heeeeeee!
Owen Oh, for God's sake.
Mara I'm going to tuck my feet up. (*She does so, and turns to face Angel, so that she is leaning against Hilberto. To Angel*) Now tell me about the beginning of your childhood. Tell me the very first thing you can remember.
Owen Are we all allowed to take notes?
Mara No, you two can just quietly check through your notes on the new town. (*To Hilberto*) Can you drive with me leaning against you?
Angel *¿ Puedes conducir asi ?*
Hilberto (*grinning*) *Me arreglaré de alguna manera.*
Angel He says, he will manage somehow.
Owen Oh come on, or all the mango-juice will have gone.

The foreground Lights go down. The sky turns to the orange and flame of a tropical sunset

Scene 8

The table is placed downstage, with four of the chairs around it. The other two chairs are upstage, silhouetted against the sunset

Owen and Ed are sitting at the table with daiquiri glasses in front of them.

Owen It's so embarrassing for everyone else! That's what I object to. I mean, *I* don't care. It's not the sort of thing that worries me. But it must be a little irritating for you, mustn't it?
Ed For me?
Owen I should feel a little put out, if I were in your position.
Ed Owen, what claim do I have on Mara?

Owen I think that's a very sensible attitude to take, Ed. I admire that. If only everyone could be so forbearing. After all, you'd put in quite a lot of preliminary spadework there.

Ed I wouldn't call that preliminary spadework.

Owen It looked like preliminary spadework to me.

Ed Oh God! We're in Cuba! The sun was shining . . .

Owen Oh, sure. Nothing more natural.

Ed I didn't see that as preliminary spadework.

Owen It must be very embarrassing for Angel, though. That's what worries me.

Ed I thought he was handling the situation in the car very well.

Owen It puts him in an impossible position.

Ed Owen, these boys know how to cope with this kind of thing.

Owen But this man is the official spokesman for the Cuban Government! No official government spokesman wants to be asked to tell the story of his life!

Ed Owen, I have news for you. Everyone wants to be asked to tell the story of his life.

Owen Yes, but not while some lady novelist rumples his hair!

Ed I'd tell the story of my life while some lady novelist rumpled my hair.

Owen Look at them.

Angel and Mara enter. They look around for somewhere to sit

Poor Angel. He doesn't know where to put himself.

Angel and Mara look in their direction. Owen smilingly pulls out chairs and indicates that they should sit at the table

Are we going to have to sit at the same table all evening, watching her make eyes at him?

Mara gives a little wave to Ed and Owen, then takes Angel by the arm and leads him to the two chairs upstage

Ed Answer: no, we're not going to have to sit at the same table all evening, watching her make eyes at him.

Owen That's what is technically known as Government circles being wheeled around up there.

Ed He looks a little dizzy.

Owen He looks like that pull-along duck Hilberto got hold of.

Ed Anyway, don't worry about him. He can handle it.

Mara and Angel turn the two chairs so that they face upstage, and sit looking into the sunset, two silhouettes

Owen It's so *unprofessional*! If there's one moral quality in life I do actually care about, it's professionalism.
Ed Owen, she's not *in* your profession! She's a fiction writer.
Owen Fiction writer! We're all going to be bloody fiction writers by the time this lot's over. That's virtually our only source of information out there having his arm squeezed.

Mara is leaning towards Angel, murmuring to him and touching his arm

Ed The sight of them out there in the twilight does bring it all back. (*He laughs*)
Owen Does bring all what back?

Ed laughs

What?

Ed laughs

Long-lost summer nights in Urbana, Illinois?
Ed (*shaking his head and laughing*) Doesn't it disturb you at all?
Owen Me? Oh, I'm married.
Ed I'm married.
Owen I shouldn't want to go back to that stage.
Ed Never knowing what was going to happen next.
Owen It always gave me indigestion.
Ed It gave me a reason for existence.

They look at Angel and Mara

Owen (*disturbed*) Oh, shit!
Ed It's the twilight.
Owen It's the warmth.
Ed It's the scent of the night.
Owen *Shit!*
Ed No, the thing is, when I was here a couple of years back, they gave me a girl to show me round.
Owen And?

Ed turns and looks at Angel and Mara, then turns back. He sighs

I see.

Ed I wrote to her afterwards. I must have written six or seven times. Not a word. Then one of the Canadian food and agriculture people here told me she'd got married.

Owen You still think about her?

Ed At times.

Owen Yes.

Ed In places.

Owen I know what you mean.

Mara and Angel laugh privately at something. She puts her head against his arm

Ed I'll tell you one thing, though. I wrote the best damned piece about this country afterwards that *I've* ever seen printed.

Owen looks round restlessly

What?

Owen The girl behind the bar.

Ed The one with the ass?

Owen She's not too bad.

Ed You're interested, are you?

Owen Do you think she speaks English?

Ed She doesn't look the kind of person who speaks English.

Owen I suppose you could translate.

Ed I suppose I could.

Owen I suppose not.

Ed I suppose you could manage without language, couldn't you?

Owen What, smile? Raise my eyebrows?

Ed And so on.

Owen Then *she* smiles, and raises *her* eyebrows?

Ed And so forth.

Owen I'll get a hell of an article out of that.

Ed I suppose *I* could talk to her.

Owen I suppose you could.

Ed You don't regard yourself as having any prior claim, do you? Since you put in the preliminary spadework?

Owen Preliminary spadework?

Ed Preliminary intellectual spadework.

Owen (*gloomily*) No, go ahead. Plant your potatoes.
Ed If I make any headway, I'll ask her whether she's got a friend.
Owen Do that.
Ed A friend who speaks English.
Owen With dark, mysterious eyes.
Ed If she has, I'll look across at you and smile, like that.
Owen And raise your eyebrows twice.
Ed Like that.
Owen Otherwise I'll see you at breakfast tomorrow.
Ed It's a deal.

Ed exits

Angel and Mara laugh quietly together

Owen *Shit!*

The foreground Lights go down. The sky becomes completely dark as the foreground Lights come up for the next scene

Scene 9

As in Scene 4, there are four separate pools of light on different parts of the set. In the two outer areas, Owen and Ed sit on the edge of raised levels, each with a typewriter on the chair in front of him. In one of the two inner areas, Hilberto is cleaning the shovel he traded; in the other, Mara is lying on the raised level and Angel is sitting on the chair

Owen and Ed are both leaning gloomily over their typewriters but failing to type

Cicadas

Owen kicks off his shoes. Ed wipes his face and unbuttons his shirt. Owen unbuttons his shirt and wipes his face.

Angel And yet to be superior to others is not so easy, I think. My father he laughed at the men in the factory who liked to do things they cannot afford. But my father he also liked to do things he cannot afford. He liked to eat. He liked to buy medicine when we were sick. So my poor father must take another job in the evenings also. He must be not only a financier but also a musician. He must work with playing the violin in a Hungarian Gypsy band. In this Hungarian Gypsy band are three men: my father with his violin; Mr Alvarez the postman with his accordion; and a man with spectacles who sings the Gypsy songs and plays the maraccas. Why, in a Hungarian Gypsy band, they have maraccas—this I never discover. But they dress themselves as Hungarian Gypsies, and they go to all the tables in the hotel, and they serenade the people who are eating their dinner. Which hotel? In our town is only one hotel. Who are these people they serenade? They are not the men who make the shoes. They serenade the chief of police and his wife. They serenade the local railroad manager and his wife. They serenade the man who has the Chrysler automobile agency and the man who has the Westinghouse electric agency. And when my father comes home he tells us about them. "These people!" he says. "These people!" "What do you think? Mr Valdes lost two thousand pesos on the horses last week! Just imagine, Mr Castañeda is sending his son to New York for a year to learn merchandising!" And he laughs. But now he laughs in a different way. Because these people have big ideas that cost not hundreds of pesos like the big ideas of the men who make the shoes but thousands of pesos, and tens of thousands of pesos. And if there is one thing that my father respects in life it is three zeros together. And sometimes, if he is in a good mood, he takes me to look at these people so that I shall know what the world is like. He brings me through the kitchens and lets me hide in a balcony above the dining-room. I look down—and there is the famous Mr Valdes and the terrible Mr Castañeda. There is Mrs Valdes eating steak tartare. There is Mrs Castañeda, who is not Mrs Castañeda at all, putting yet more lipstick on her scarlet lips. And I think—so this is what the world is like! Everything good and everything bad is here. If it is permitted to me, if I work hard and behave myself well, this is the world I shall grow up to live in. But my poor father! One night while I am watching, there come some strange people. Brazilians, with some American friends. Rich people. Why have they come to our small town? There is nothing there for travellers to see. But they like it there. Yes, they like it greatly. It makes them laugh to be in such a town. They laugh and they laugh. It is the most comical place they have ever visited. They laugh at Mr Valdes. They laugh at Mrs Castañeda. They laugh at the Hungarian Gypsies with the maraccas. They laugh at my father. At the end of each song they clap very loudly and they shout "Bravo!" and "Encore!" And they give money to the band to play again. I think never does my father receive so much money. And as I watch I understand that after all my father knows nothing. He is nobody. He says "These people!" but he is himself only "these people". I understand that this hotel is not after all the world. This town is not the world. This country is not the world. The world is in other places.

Mara This is where the world is now.
Angel Now many things have changed.
Mara It's not to laugh that people come here these days.
Angel I think that some people do not come here to laugh.

Pause. Owen rips off his shirt, wipes his face with it, and throws it aside. Once again he is distracted by the voices just as he is about to type

Mara Does Hilberto have a friend in this place?
Angel In this place also he has a friend.
Mara Is he taking him a present?
Angel He takes her a present.
Mara Her? Are many of Hilberto's friends her?
Angel I think quite many.
Mara And she'll give him a present?
Angel She gives him a present.
Mara Soon Hilberto will be a rich man.
Angel I think this is not so. I think the present this friend gives him will not make him richer. I think tomorrow he must start again with one cigar.

Hilberto tiptoes off, holding the shovel

Owen rips off his trousers, and throws them aside

Mara Hilberto has beautiful eyes.
Angel Other people also.
Mara Such soft brown eyes everywhere. Full of warmth and sleep.
Angel I did not mean Cuban people.
Mara Not Mr Shorter? Mr Shorter has eyes like little hard throat pastilles.
Angel I did not mean Mr Shorter or Mr Budge.

Pause

Mara I shan't laugh, Angel. I haven't come here to laugh.

Angel suddenly transfers from the chair to sit beside Mara. She gives a terrible scream, and draws away. He jumps up, aghast. Owen and Ed also jump up, no less aghast. Mara screams again

Owen Oh God!

Owen hurries towards Mara's patch of light, then notices his state of undress, and hurries back

Oh God oh God oh God oh God!

He scrambles into his trousers, but his haste delays him. Ed by this time has arrived in Mara's patch of light

Ed (*terrified*) What? What?
Mara Touched me!
Ed Touched you?
Mara Touched my leg! Horrible! Slimy! Eyes—bulging! Throat going throb, throb!
Ed (*indicating Angel*) Him?
Mara (*pointing at where she was sitting*) That!

They look. There is a frog sitting on the bed

Ed The frog?
Mara Jumped!
Ed The frog touched you?
Mara Out of the dark! Out of nowhere!
Ed (*to Angel*) Frog.
Angel I take it away.

Angel goes off with the frog

Mara I'm sorry.
Ed You don't like frogs?
Mara I don't mind frogs.
Ed It was probably a prince in disguise.
Mara I thought it was a snake.
Ed A snake?
Mara Flop! And there was something cold and dark on my leg.
Ed It's snakes you're worried about, is it, Mara?
Mara I'm not worried about snakes. It was thinking it was a snake, and then seeing it was a snake that looked like a frog.
Ed Sleep well, Mara.
Mara Have you ever seen a snake with bulging eyes and a throat going throb, throb?
Ed And if you don't feel better in the morning, remember there's a fine health service here.

Ed goes back to his area of light. Owen, who has also stopped to drag his shirt back on and to stuff his feet into his shoes, runs into Mara's patch of light

Owen (*in a state of alarm*) What? What?
Mara (*alarmed by his alarm*) What?
Owen What is it?
Mara "What is it?" What's what?
Owen What?
Mara What?
Owen What do you mean, "what?"? You were screaming!
Mara Oh. Then.
Owen What were you screaming about?
Mara There was a frog on my bed.
Owen A *frog*?
Mara What did you think it was?
Owen What did I think it was? I didn't stop to think! You were screaming the hotel down! A frog! My God! After this little trip I shudder to think what kind of reputation the British press is going to have abroad! It's an absolute bloody disgrace to the newspaper industry to send someone like you out here on a job like this! You sulk—you weep—you embarrass Government officials. And now you scream your head off because you've seen a frog! I thought you were being raped!

Mara You thought I was being raped?
Owen For all I knew!
Mara You certainly took your time, then! It would all have been over by the time you got here!

They gaze at each other in fury

Owen Well, I must say! That's the last time I ever come to *your* aid!

He marches back to his own area, and stands there, rigid with anger

Angel returns to Mara's area

Suddenly, Mara's anger disappears. She laughs

Angel What?
Mara I've only just realized.

She crosses to Owen's area

(*Gently*) You are a fool. Next time I scream, please don't stop to get dressed.

She kisses him on the cheek, and returns to her own area. She and Angel sit down as before. Owen remains standing. Then, abruptly, he takes a mirror out of his shirt pocket, and begins to smoothe his hair into place

CURTAIN

ACT II

Scene 1

Once again the sky is full of cumulus. No table, no chairs

Owen and Mara

Owen Funny.
Mara When?
Owen In the hatchery.
Mara Oh, in the hatchery.
Owen On and on he went.
Mara Like a lawnmower in the distance.
Owen A thousand chicks a week.
Mara A thousand chicks a day.
Owen A week.
Mara A day.
Owen You weren't listening.
Mara You weren't listening.
Owen I was listening.
Mara You were walking round in a daze.
Owen You don't know what I was doing.
Mara I was watching you.
Owen You weren't watching me.
Mara How do you know I wasn't watching you?
Owen Because I was watching you.
Mara So I noticed.
Owen Funny.
Mara When?
Owen When we both looked at each other at the same time.
Mara Quite funny.
Owen And then you knew?
Mara Oh, I knew before.
Owen When?
Mara As soon as I saw you.
Owen In the Ministry of External Relations?
Mara You smiled.

Owen And you knew?
Mara I knew.
Owen I didn't know.
Mara I know you didn't.
Owen I didn't know you liked me.
Mara You didn't even know you liked me.
Owen No, I didn't know.
Mara *Buenos dias*.
Owen What?
Mara What you said.
Owen When?
Mara Then.
Owen *I* said?
Mara Stupid thing to say.
Owen *You* said!
Mara You.
Owen I said good morning.
Mara Not much to boast about.
Owen But you knew?
Mara I knew.
Owen And you knew that you liked me?
Mara I knew.
Owen I thought it was Angel you liked. Well, first I thought it was Ed. Then I thought it was Angel.
Mara I thought, what, do I have to flirt with the entire male population of Cuba before he shows any interest? I thought, God, do I have to scream the entire island down?
Owen I thought that was the frog.
Mara You.
Owen No frog?
Mara Oh, there was a *frog*. Just there was no you.
Owen I see.
Mara So then you knew.
Owen Then I knew. Lay awake all night.
Mara Funny.
Owen When?
Mara At breakfast this morning. The way you looked at me.
Owen How did I look at you?
Mara Like a sleepwalker.
Owen How I felt.

Mara Without seeing me.
Owen I saw you.
Mara Funny.
Owen When?
Mara In the hatchery.
Owen But you knew already?
Mara I knew.
Owen I knew, really.
Mara You knew?
Owen As soon as you walked through that door and said *Buenos dias*.
Mara I said it? You said it!
Owen I said good morning.
Mara You don't remember anything.
Owen I remember everything.
Mara Everything?
Owen Every word. Every look.
Mara You were so bloody to me.
Owen Yes.
Mara That mango-juice.
Owen Yes.
Mara Five weeks to get to London.
Owen Yes.
Mara Labour wards.
Owen Labour camps.
Mara Work camps.
Owen Everything I did.
Mara Why were you so bloody to me?
Owen Trying to stop it happening.
Mara Didn't you want it to happen?
Owen I'm married.
Mara Everyone's married.
Owen Are you married?
Mara Everyone's married.
Owen It's not as if I don't love my wife. Because I do. I do.
Mara I know you do.
Owen I do. I do.
Mara I'm glad you do.
Owen I mean, I really do.
Mara But.

Owen No, I honestly do.
Mara But.
Owen No.
Mara Anyway.
Owen So.
Mara So?
Owen So I was bloody to you. Do you think the others know about us?
Mara How?
Owen Noticed something.
Mara Nothing to notice.
Owen Only that we vanished somewhere between the hatcheries and the piggeries.
Mara Oh. Always vanishing.
Owen You were.
Mara Sitting in the shade.
Owen You. Not me.
Mara No, not you.
Owen Slaving in the sun, I was.
Mara I felt so terrible, Owen.
Owen *I* always used to be homesick on these trips.
Mara I didn't know whether I was there any more. I didn't know whether it was still me or whether it was some leaden-hearted stranger.
Owen You should have said.
Mara No-one I could say it to.
Owen Ed, Angel.
Mara I thought they looked down on me. I thought they looked right through me and saw nothing.
Owen Always me.
Mara You?
Owen You knew how I felt about you.
Mara *You* didn't know how you felt about me.
Owen *You* knew.
Mara What does anyone know about anything?
Owen Days wasted!
Mara Days to come.
Owen Four.
Mara Four good days.
Owen Who knows?

Mara Four long days.
Owen Who knows anything?
Mara Four days and nights.
Owen They went off to the piggeries hours ago.
Mara Think of them all out there.
Owen Walking round in the sun.
Mara And only Ed to enjoy it.
Owen Poor Ed.
Mara Think you should be out there with him?
Owen He's doing the work of three.
Mara Feel bad about it?
Owen Asking all the questions.
Mara Go and join them.
Owen Taking an interest in the pigs.
Mara Don't stay here if you're going to feel bad about it.
Owen Look at the clouds.
Mara No piggeries there.
Owen No piggeries, no pigs, no people.
Mara I can see *you*.
Owen Where?
Mara Up there. The one with the anxious look on its face. The one with that great tangle of white hair.
Owen I haven't got white hair.
Mara I like you with white hair.
Owen It's not me.
Mara It's you.
Owen How do you know?
Mara I know. You've got your children with you. And I suppose that's your wife. She looks nice.
Owen She is nice.
Mara Ranges of cloud. Bank upon bank. You look at clouds like that in a certain light and you see some strange familiarity. Other days in other years and other places. Days you half-remember from some other life.
Owen I always see London. London on certain afternoons in the forties. London in the early years of the nineteenth century, before the railways were built. You'd walk out of the city on dusty white roads, and come into a muddled countryside of sheds and small market gardens somewhere just beyond King's Cross.

Mara I like the district you live in. It's spring—there's flowering cherry all along the street. Pages of newspapers swirling and scurrying along a parade of shops, catching in brambles and hawthorns on a little common. Now it's summer. Behind the houses the allotments are head-high with beans. Between the houses the entries are choked in rank cow-parsley and elderberry. God, the smell of the cow-parsley on summer afternoons! The smell of the creosote on the fences! You can't help thinking how strange and familiar England is. And how fine. When you see it up there. I should think you're very happy in a place like that. But I don't know. Your children are getting bigger all the time. You're all spreading out, moving away from each other into open blue sky. And you've got a strange look on your face. You're turning slowly round with a kind of lop-sided smile, as if it's all still a mystery to you after all. You're going up to another man who's also got a mystified, lop-sided smile on his face. You're leaning on each other. You're both rather drunk, I think, and you're holding each other up. You're trying to explain to each other how mystifying life has turned out to be. But not a sound does either of you manage to utter. You're performing this slow, smiling dance together in a white silence. And very gradually you're sinking down on to your knees and disintegrating.

Owen I don't get drunk.

Mara You should.

Owen I'm not disintegrating yet.

Mara You will.

Owen I can see you, too.

Mara Which one is me?

Owen The one with the white scarf trailing in the wind. The one driving the open car.

Mara Where am I driving to?

Owen To Brescia. Or perhaps to Vicenza. Or across the frontier, and on to Zagreb. You haven't decided. You're coming from Geneva.

Mara Why did I leave Geneva?

Owen A man.

Mara Why am I going to Bresica?

Owen A man.

Mara Is there also a man in Vicenza?

Owen And in Zagreb.
Mara I can see them. Just. Far away over the Sierra. White-haired men like you.
Owen Men of depth and distinction.
Mara How altogether deep and distinguished Europe looks up there!
Owen All that money. All that past.
Mara Filling-stations with ten thousand plastic spinners spinning in the wind.
Owen Towns famous for nougat.
Mara Delivery trucks in the shape of giant toothpaste tubes.
Owen Ski-lifts.
Mara Strange, delicately coloured banknotes.
Owen Brescia.
Mara Vicenza.

Angel enters

Angel (*to Mara*) Oh. You are here.
Mara Tell us about the pigs.
Angel I looked for you in many places. But you are here?
Mara I am here. Here is where I always am.
Angel You are feeling unwell? (*He takes her hand*)
Mara I'm feeling well. Here also is Mr Shorter.

Angel sees Owen. He releases Mara's hand

Angel Oh.
Owen And I also am feeling well. I hope you made our excuses to the pigs.
Angel I think now you are fully rested we must come back to the car.
Owen Where are we off to now?
Mara Vicenza.
Owen Brescia.
Mara King's Cross.
Angel I think now we must go to the experimental fertilizer plant.

The foreground Lights go down

Scene 2

Car and sky

Hilberto is asleep on the ground. Ed is standing looking at him

Owen enters

Owen (*looking at Hilberto*) Cuba.
Ed Right.
Owen Beautiful.
Ed When I went out at six this morning, he was coming in.
Owen With his shovel?
Ed Without his shovel.
Owen Shovel all night, sleep all day. (*He laughs*) You're right, Ed. These people have got the secret of life. How did *your* night's shovelling go, by the way?
Ed My night's shovelling?
Owen Your piece of spadework.
Ed Oh. She doesn't finish in the bar until eleven. And she's married to one of the boys in the alfalfa meal plant down the road.
Owen Oh.
Ed We had quite an interesting talk about alfalfa, though. Hey, Owen, you're right about our mutual lady-friend. She's in quite a state.
Owen Oh. I didn't really mean all that. I got a little carried away.
Ed A frog!
Owen In the case of the frog, I think the thing was, she thought it was a snake.
Ed A jumping snake!
Owen I think honestly that's what startled her—the snake behaving like a frog.
Ed It *was* a frog!
Owen I think that was really the trouble.
Ed Anyway, thanks for keeping her occupied this afternoon.
Owen Oh. Any time.
Ed No, it really worked. I had Angel all to myself, and I got some fantastic stuff out of him. We sat down in back of the

hog-pens there with one or two of the hogmen, and we just talked.

Owen About hogs?

Ed Hogs and hogmen. Hogs, hogmen, and hogbiz. Great stuff. Angel has an uncle on his mother's side who's into hogs. Some of the stories he told! I could write a book! Well, I am writing a book. How did you keep Mary Jane occupied? Ask her to step into the sugar cane and look at your etchings?

Owen I shouldn't put it quite like that.

Ed No, I know your feelings about the lady, so have a cigar to make up. (*He offers a box*) No, go on—I don't smoke. They're a present from the farm chairman.

Owen takes one

Here they come. But don't worry. Because now we have a plan, and the plan is we take her turn and turn about.

Owen Ed, I don't think we need any plans.

Ed No, you can knock off now, because I'm on duty.

Owen You go on talking to Angel.

Ed You get in there with Angel.

Owen I think I know how to cope with Mara.

Ed I think I know how to cope with Mara. I'm going to gaze into her eyes and tell her I've always secretly been in love with her.

Angel and Mara enter

Angel, have a cigar.

Angel (*shaking his head*) Thank you. I have trouble, here.

Ed You have trouble. Anyone else like a cigar?

Hilberto wakes up

Mara, you have an appreciation of the finer things of life. Come and sit next to me in the back of our chaffeur-driven Cadillac and smoke a very large cigar, and imagine you're sitting in the back of a chauffeur-driven Cadillac smoking a very large cigar.

Angel I think Miss Hill should like to sit in the front and stretch her legs.

Ed All right. We'll sit in front and stretch our legs. (*He ushers Mara in*)

Mara But perhaps Owen would like to sit in front and stretch his legs?

Owen Why not? Then Ed could stretch out in the back and get some sleep, after all his exertions in the piggeries.

Ed No, no. I'll stretch my legs in front, and you stretch out in the back.

Owen You stretch out. I'll stretch my legs.

Ed (*puzzled*) Owen, I thought we agreed it was my turn to . . . stretch my legs?

Angel To end the argument, I think I stretch my legs.

Angel gets in the front next to Mara. Mara gets out the other side

Mara Or alternatively I could go in the back, since I've got the shortest legs.

Mara gets in the back

Ed That makes sense. (*To Owen*) O.K., then, *you* stretch your legs with Angel. (*He starts to get in the back*)

Owen Ed, hold on a minute.

Ed What?

Owen I think Hilberto would like a cigar. I think after all that shovelling Hilberto *needs* a cigar.

Ed Hilberto, I'm deeply sorry.

Ed turns to Hilberto and offers him the box

Hilberto (*taking one*) *Gracias. ¿ Me permites?* (*His hand hovers*)

Ed Take two. Take three. Take the whole box. (*He gives it to him*) *Son tuyos, amigo mio.*

Ed turns to get into the back of the car. But Owen is already sitting there, beside Mara, and is somehow occupying all the available space

Owen Get in somewhere, Ed. You'll be left behind.

Puzzled, Ed gets into the front beside Angel. Hilberto gets into the driving-seat

Mara A whole box! I wonder what condition he's going to be in by the time he gets back to his wife.

Angel (*stony faced*) I wonder many things.

Hilberto drives. They all jerk back a little as the car starts, then bounce up and down as it drives over a rough track. Angel continues dour; Ed thoughtful. Mara and Hilberto are in good spirits; Owen in ridiculously good spirits. They all keel over as the car makes a turn on to the open road, and the bouncing ceases

Owen (*in an American accent*) And so we bid a reluctant farewell to the Collective Farm "Victory of Communism", home of fine Cuban bacon. (*Speaking normally, his hand on Ed's shoulder*) Sorry, Ed. Forgot you were here. (*He makes a self-deprecating face at Mara*). No, seriously, I really enjoyed the visit. I found it both illuminating and stimulating. Thank you for bringing us, Angel. Where next? Did you say it was an experimental sewage farm?

Angel (*stonily*) An experimental fertilizer plant.

Owen An experimental fertilizer plant. Of course. As a matter of fact I'm rather looking forward to it. (*To Mara*) Are you looking forward to it?

Mara I *am* rather looking forward to it.

Owen I'm rather more than rather looking forward to it. I'm greatly looking forward to it.

Mara You're immensely looking forward to it.

Owen No, not immensely. I find it difficult to know exactly how much. Not immensely, though. (*He puts his hand on Angel's shoulder*) But greatly, Angel, greatly.

Mara Angel doesn't think you're serious.

Owen Turn round, Angel. I can't see the expression on your face.

Angel turns his head minimally, with a minimal smile.

Mara (*to Owen*) He's not convinced.

Owen Angel, don't misunderstand us! We think this country is the greatest place on earth! (*To Mara*) Don't we?

Mara Look at those buzzards. Wheeling. Wheeling.

Owen Look at that little kid with the week's washing balanced on her head!

Mara Look at the clouds. Shifting. Shifting.

Owen Soon you'll control the weather. Then the clouds will be yours.

Mara Towering cities of snow and bronze.

Owen Clouds to order.
Mara Sugar and coffee.
Owen The new man and the new clouds.
Mara The new world, coming in on the Trades.
Owen Look at that old boy on the donkey! Big cigar! Fat as a film producer! (*He puts his hand on Angel's shoulder*) Angel, this is a great country you've got here!
Angel (*with a wan smile*) Thank you.
Mara Angel, we love your country! (*She kisses him*)
Angel I am pleased that you like it.
Owen We don't just like it, Angel—we love it. I say that with tears in my eyes. (*To Mara*) Will you testify that I have genuine tears in my eyes?
Mara He has tears in one eye.
Owen No, seriously, we all love it. Ed loves it. (*To Ed*) Don't you just love this cute little old island? (*He puts his hand on Ed's shoulder*) Sorry, Ed. Sorry. Slipped out. But you do love Cuba, don't you?
Ed (*sombrely*) *I* do. But then I always have. Unlike some people.
Owen Ed, there's more joy in Havana over one sinner that repenteth than over nine and ninety just men. How are you getting along there behind the wheel, Hilberto? This is ridiculous! I've scarcely spoken to Hilberto since the trip began. How are you, Hilberto? *¿Como estás, amigo?*
Hilberto (*cheerfully*) *¡Estupendo!*
Owen (*clapping Hilberto on the back*) *¡Estupendo!* That's the way to be!
Hilberto Whee—heeeeee!
Owen Whoo—hoooooo!
Mara And we say that in all seriousness.

The foreground Lights go down

Scene 3

The table is in the centre. All six chairs are in a straight line along one side of the room

Angel is sitting on the table. Ed is pacing up and down

Ed I'm hungry.

Silence

I need a drink. I need a shower. We all want to cram as much as possible into the day. But there's a limit.

Silence

Hilberto must have found them by now. Fantastic, isn't it? Suddenly they're interested in something. We look at sugar mills, we look at new towns, we look at power stations, and that pair can scarcely trouble themselves to get out of the car. Then all of a sudden, at the end of a long day when some of us have been working, they discover an insatiable interest in the development of new fertilizers.

Angel I think I do not understand.

Ed I don't understand. They're supposed to be in competition with each other. I should have thought this was highly unprofessional.

Angel Many times he complains me about her. Many times she complains me about him.

Ed You must feel pretty sore.

Angel I have no personal feelings in this matter.

Ed But it's so damned unfair! If it was me, I could go and sock him in the mouth. But you're a Government official. Your job is to look after him.

Angel My personal feelings are not important.

Ed Or perhaps you *could* sock him. Could you? Or would that be a breach of labour discipline? This could be an interesting legal point.

Angel There is no question, if I should hit anyone.

Ed I've seen this happen time and time again. That's what saddens me. People go off on some jamboree like this, and they think, right, seven days away from wife and children, and woof!—they start to fool around. They behave like kids necking at the back of the bus on a high school outing. And, sure enough, somebody gets hurt.

Angel I worry only that I think we do not now get any dinner.

Ed We've all got wives. We've all got children. There they are, sitting at home, thinking about us, wondering what we're doing, worrying about us. And here we are, worrying and wondering about them. Some of us. And some of us apparently not. Some of us not worrying or wondering at all.

Angel My wife works also for the Ministry of External Relations. She is now in province of Oriente with a delegation of Italian journalists.

Hilberto enters on all fours, backwards. Mara and Owen follow him

Mara A donkey?
Owen A pig?
Mara A mouse?
Owen A man on all fours?

Hilberto lowers his head and charges them

Mara A bull!
Owen He was a bullfighter!
Mara *¿Torero?*

Hilberto shakes his head, and bleats

Owen Sheep?
Mara A sheepfighter?

Hilberto springs about on all fours

Owen A mule!
Mara A mule! A mule! A mule!
Owen He was a mule-driver!
Mara You were a mule-driver?
Owen He was a mule-driver with Castro when they were fighting in the mountains.
Hilberto *¡Castro! ¡Si! ¡Castro! ¡Castro!*
Mara We've got there.
Owen We've done it.
Angel I think now we must quickly go, please.
Mara Angel, we love Hilberto!
Owen We've had the most astonishing conversation with him!
Mara He's told us his entire life story!
Ed Good. Now can we go and eat?
Owen (*to Ed*) Cuba. You were right. He is.
Mara And he's a great man.

Owen (*to Hilberto*) Mule-driver! With Castro!
Hilberto *¡Castro! ¡Si, si!*

Hilberto gets down on his hands and knees again. He bares his teeth and snaps them open and closed

Owen Oh, there's more to come. What's this, then?
Ed He's hungry. He wants his dinner.
Mara He *was* hungry. In the mountains.
Owen Or he ate something.
Mara There wasn't anything to eat.
Owen He ate the mule.
Angel I think we go.
Ed You can finish the story over dinner.

Hilberto laughs, and acts a large-scale demonstration of madness

Owen He can't tell this bit at dinner.
Mara What's he saying?
Owen He's saying he was mad.
Mara He was mad with hunger.
Owen He was mad with joy. Look, he's laughing.
Mara That's insane laughter.
Owen Yes, he was insane with delight. When Castro won.
Mara He was mad with hunger. When they ate the mule.
Owen (*to Angel*) Ask him. Was he mad with hunger, or was he mad with joy?
Angel (*to Hilberto*) *¿Les cuentas aquello de tu tía abuela?*
Hilberto *Si.*
Angel He tells about the sister of his grandmother.
Owen Was she a mule-driver?
Angel She was a nun.
Mara And what was she doing with this mule?
Angel It was a goat.
Owen A goat. Of course.
Mara And she ate the goat?
Angel The goat bite her.
Owen Oh. And she went mad?
Angel The goat went mad.
Mara Of course.
Angel He tells a joke.

Hilberto does a reprise of the mad scene

Owen He told it very well.

Hilberto laughs, and gets to his feet

Mara Hilberto, you're sweet! (*She puts her arm round him*)
Angel I hear this joke many times.
Mara Angel, you're sweet, too. (*She puts her other arm round Angel*)
Owen Just a moment. How does Castro come into the story?
Angel *¿Castro?*
Hilberto *¡Sí! ¡Castro!*
Angel *Castro* means in Spanish when you go to the little house where the bees live, and you take out the honey.
Owen I see—So Hilberto's grandmother's sister went to the little house where the bees live . . .
Mara . . . in her nun's habit . . .
Owen . . . and her beekeeper's mask . . .
Mara . . . and bent down . . .
Angel . . . and the goat bite her.
Mara *¿Castro?*
Angel *Castrŏ.*
Mara Taking honey from the bees.
Owen Which is exactly what Fidel is doing!
Mara And giving it to these two. Come on. The roast mule will be getting dry.

Mara exits with Angel and Hilberto,

Ed (*sourly*) Sweet!
Owen Don't you think so?
Ed What? That two grown, self-respecting men are sweet?
Owen That everything here is sweet? That life is sweet?
Ed *Sweet?* Like sugar?
Owen Yes, like sugar.
Ed Like sugar, that's right. And you've seen how sugar's produced. By back-breaking labour under the sun.
Owen It's sweet, all the same.
Ed The labour?
Owen The sugar. And life. And you.

They go off

The foreground Lights go down. Night falls as the Lights come up for the next scene

SCENE 4

Four separate areas of light, as in Scenes 4 and 9 in the first act. In the two outer areas sit Angel and Ed; in the two inner ones Owen and Mara

Angel, Ed and Owen have typewriters on their chairs. Angel lights a cigarette and gazes into space, lost in bitter reflection. Mara is curled up on the raised level which represents her bed, and is writing by hand at great speed. Ed is tapping his fingers on the top of his typewriter impatiently. But each time he is about to type something he is distracted by the sound of Owen typing

Cicadas

Owen types a final sentence, then winds the paper up in the machine to read it

Owen Friday. Max. temp. eighty-seven. Wind NW. Cloudy. Visit Collective Farm "Victory of Communism". Inspect maize, carrots, and lucerne. Chairman explains how yields have been increased by up to eighty per cent since collectivization. Have impression he is telling truth. Members of collective have apparently volunteered to work two hours' unpaid overtime each day, in order to achieve production targets laid down in five-year plan. Feel from atmosphere that this enthusiasm probably quite genuine. Excellent lunch. Fresh mango-juice. After lunch visit hatchery. In hatchery find out much that did not know. (*He stops and smiles to himself*) After hatchery inspect sugar cane. Long talk about life with Mara. (*He thinks. Then winds the paper down, xms out the last sentence, and types another*) Short chat about the clouds with Miss Hill. (*He deletes this in its turn, and types another sentence*) Endless conversation about the weather with our distinguished lady novelist.

He rips the paper out of the machine in disgust, and goes next door to see Mara. She looks up and smiles, then continues to write. He watches her

Mara What?
Owen You.
Mara And you.
Owen I mean, writing.
Mara At last.
Owen But so much.
Mara So much happened.
Owen Too much.
Mara Too much?
Owen Too much to take in. Too much to put down.
Mara Have you finished?
Owen No.
Mara Once I start I never stop.
Owen I can't start.
Mara What's the problem?
Owen You.
Mara Oh.
Owen Can't write about you.
Mara Then don't write about me.
Owen Can't not write about you.
Mara Then write about me.

Owen sighs

Don't have to send it home.
Owen No.
Mara Not every word you write.
Owen No.
Mara Read out by your children over breakfast.
Owen I suppose not.
Mara Not your whole life.
Owen But in the actual piece . . .
Mara Write about me.
Owen I can't!
Mara Why not?
Owen In the piece?
Mara In the piece.
Owen It's not professional!
Mara People have written about me.
Owen To write about the opposition.
Mara Also they deliver the paper at home.

Owen There's that, too.
Mara Your children read it out over breakfast.
Owen They might.
Mara So write about fertilizer instead.

Owen sighs. He goes back to his own area, sits down at his typewriter, winds a sheet of paper into it, without a carbon, and types two or three words. Then he thinks, and returns to Mara's area

Owen Are you writing about fertilizer?
Mara Yes.
Owen Are you writing about Hilberto eating the mule?
Mara Of course.

Owen returns to his own area and sits down in front of the typewriter. He thinks

Owen (*calling*) The buzzards?
Mara Certainly.
Owen The clouds?
Mara Everything.

Owen goes to Mara's area and watches her writing

Owen Look, we must pool our resources. We must work out some way of sharing the material between us.
Mara Different buzzards.
Owen How do you mean?
Mara Your buzzards won't come out like my buzzards. The clouds you see aren't the clouds I see.
Owen Possibly not.
Mara We can share the world and still have a world each.
Owen But will they see it like that in the office?
Mara They'll see it like that if you see it like that.
Owen I wonder.
Mara Either you make people see the world the way you do, or they make you see the world the way they do.
Owen Are you writing about me?
Mara Yes.
Owen What about me?
Mara Everything about you.
Owen My name?
Mara Your initial.

Owen O?
Mara Every page looks like a bag of holes.
Owen But in the piece . . .?
Mara I'll change it to A.
Owen They read it at home, of course.
Mara The children?
Owen Everyone.
Mara Over breakfast?
Owen They won't be fooled by A.
Mara Never mind. Perhaps tomorrow we'll get separate cars . . .

Silence

Solve the problem.

Silence

Every day Angel phones and asks.

Silence

Isn't that what you want?

Silence

Opposite ends of the island?

Owen sinks to his knees, hides his head against the floor, and utters a thin, despairing noise

What do you want, Owen?
Owen Want you.
Mara Then I have to be part of your world. And you have to be part of my world.

The click of a light switch, and Hilberto is standing in his own area of light, facing upstage

Hilberto. Spent all his cigars already.

Hilberto throws down the box of cigars

I wonder if he ever worries about it?

Hilberto sinks to his knees, hides his head against the floor, and utters a low roar of anguish. Ed and Angel listen. Owen sits up. Hilberto roars again. Mara crosses to Hilberto's area. She stands watching him

Goat?

Hilberto groans

Cow?

Hilberto groans. Owen crosses into Hilberto's area

Man in love?

Hilberto gets slowly to his feet and turns round. He is holding a bloodstained handkerchief to one eye, and there are bloodstains all over the front of his shirt

Oh, Hilberto! (*She puts her arm around him*) What happened? Was it her? Or was it the husband?

Hilberto *Las costillas.*

Mara The father? The brother?

Hilberto *Las rodillas.*

Mara Or did you just fall off the ladder?

Hilberto *Las rodillas y las costillas.*

Mara At least you hung on to the cigars. (*To Owen, who is watching in great unease*) Don't worry, love. Perhaps you'll never get caught.

The foreground Lights go down. The sky lightens to a sulphurous yellow

Scene 5

Car and sky

Hilberto is driving—in a clean shirt, but with a sticking-plaster above one eye. Next to him sit Mara and Owen. Ed and Angel are in the back. All of them except Hilberto are struggling with sleep. Eyes gaze vacantly ahead, then close irresistibly. Suddenly, a head will slump forwards or backwards. At once its proprietor will jerk it back into its upright position and start thinking aloud to stay awake

Mara Chapter Seven. That afternoon the heat grew worse. It lay upon the foothills of the sierra as thick as hot butter. The road ahead of the car liquefied into a river of molten tar and quicksilver mirages, and the air that blew through the open windows oppressed her like the breath of lions, until her eyes dissolved.

Angel I think today we must travel one hundred and twenty-seven miles. I think to obtain another car I must make telephone call from hotel one hundred and twenty-seven times. I think that the average wage for women employed in the production of artificial fertilizer is one hundred and twenty-seven degrees Centigrade.

Owen What never ceased to fascinate me, though, as we drove on and on towards Brescia, were the endlessly fascinating panoramas which never ceased to fascinate in a way which I found ceaselessly fascinating.

Ed It doesn't surprise me. Not one bit. I knew it would happen sooner or later. I knew one day we'd find ourselves driving around Cuba together again. I knew nothing would have changed.

Mara Chapter Seven. That afternoon the sky in the south grew as yellow as sulphur. She had the impression that Vicenza must be burning.

Angel I must explain you that this oppressive weather is because the air is full of Miss Hill. I must explain you that in one hundred and twenty-seven per cent of cases of sabotage in mills and warehouses during the past year the cause was found to be Miss Hill.

Ed No, no, no, it doesn't surprise me. I knew one day we'd find ourselves vacationing together in Wisconsin.

Owen What never ceased to fascinate me, though, were the panoramas of sun-warmed hair against cheek.

Mara In the south, over towards Zagreb, as the afternoon wore on, his hands grew dark in the sky, like huge thunder eye-brows brushing her cheek.

Ed Look at the cows. Those cows are typical of the hogs they raise here in Iowa.

Angel I think I must explain you that my wife understands very well how Miss Hill has set fire to the sugar crops.

Ed My wife? No, she's not here in Iowa. She's away in Cuba for the week.

Owen And everywhere I went local officials assured me that there were excellent long-term prospects of the skin just inside the front of her shirt.

Mara Chapter Seven. His hot breath stirred darkly among the sugar cane.

Owen Official statistics show that almost everyone in the country has at least two knees . . .

Mara Buzzards circled in his eyes. His clouds caressed her orchards.

Owen's head sinks on to Mara's shoulder

Owen I saw with my own eyes the plenteousness of the plum harvest.

Ed's head sinks on to Angel's shoulder

Ed God! The softness, the roundness, the warmth of all this part of the Mid-West!

Angel Isabella, I think I must explain you. This is not Miss Hill who leans on my shoulder. I think it looks like Miss Hill, Isabella. But, Isabella, I think in truth it is only Miss Hill.

Ed This is like a dream, Isabella.

Mara Chapter Eight . . .

The foreground Lights go down. The sky darkens ominously

SCENE 6

A table, with two of the chairs at it. The other four chairs are arranged in a row upstage beside the shrub

Mara sits at the table, writing. Owen sits opposite her, watching her

Distant thunder

Mara (*softly, as she writes*) Well, then. *Are* we going to, or aren't we?

Owen There's going to be such a storm in a minute. There must be. It can't go on like this.

Mara Are we or aren't we?

Owen (*getting up and walking up and down*) How does one know what to do in life?

Mara What do you want to do?
Owen How does one know what one wants to do?
Mara (*gently*) All right. Then we won't.
Owen I mean, I *want* to.
Mara Good. Then we will.
Owen Obviously I want to. Of course I want to. I assume I want to.

Pause

But I mean, it's not as though I don't love my wife, because I do.

Pause

I do. I do.

Pause

But you think we should?

Mara smiles and writes

What, now?

Mara smiles and writes.

Owen You mean . . . go to your room?
Mara Well, not the dining-room.
Owen Your room's next to Ed's room.
Mara Ed may not be there.
Owen We could go to my room.
Mara If you like.
Owen I suppose my room's next to Angel's room.
Mara Owen, what is it that's worrying you? Your wife? The others? Or something else?
Owen Nothing's worrying me. It's just that the whole thing is so . . . well, so . . .
Mara Unprofessional.
Owen All right, but I've got to go on facing them in that office for the next twenty years.
Mara (*writing*) Good night, then, love. Sleep well.

Pause

Owen Do you feel like a stroll?

Mara Through the canefields?
Owen Get a breath of air.
Mara It's going to rain.
Owen We'll have to go at once if we're going.
Mara I mean, really rain.
Owen We should have gone already.
Mara Tropical storm, Owen. Cloudburst.
Owen If we go this instant we've probably got half-an-hour.
Mara I should run, if I were you.

Pause

Owen What are you writing about? Nothing happened today.
Mara Some things happened.
Owen What things?
Mara They're still happening.
Owen You're not writing about me again?
Mara Of course.
Owen Mara, we've talked about this.
Mara Then we don't need to talk about it now.

Thunder. Owen moves round to her side of the table. Mara covers the page

What?
Owen I want to kiss your ear.
Mara You want to look over my shoulder.
Owen I want to do both.
Mara You wouldn't like what I've written.
Owen How do you know?
Mara No-one likes what's said about them.
Owen Try it on me and see.
Mara No-one likes to be pinned down in words.
Owen I'm not sensitive.
Mara Everyone's sensitive.
Owen You can say anything you like about me.
Mara I am saying anything I like about you.
Owen I just want to know what it is.
Mara You're being unprofessional.
Owen Come on.
Mara You don't show me what you've written about me.
Owen I don't write about you.

Mara Yes, you do.
Owen Certainly not.
Mara "Our distinguished lady novelist."
Owen I see. You've looked.
Mara You left it lying about.
Owen And you looked at it.
Mara You wouldn't have shown me.
Owen Of course not. Not those bits. That was before.
Mara Before?
Owen Before it all happened.
Mara And you'd show me what you wrote after?
Owen Of course.
Mara But you haven't written anything after.
Owen That's what I'm saying!
Mara Well, then!
Owen Well, then, I want to see what you're writing about me.

He tries to take the paper. Mara holds it out of reach

Look, I'm not a *buzzard*!
Mara A buzzard? Who said you were a buzzard?
Owen I mean, I'm not just part of the scenery. I'm not just a bit of local colour.
Mara (*tenderly*) Actually, you *are* a buzzard.
Owen No.
Mara An angry buzzard.
Owen I'm not a *character*!
Mara A restless, circling buzzard.
Owen I'm *me*!
Mara You look so hot, love.
Owen I *should* be me. In your eyes.
Mara As black as the sky.
Owen I want to be talked to, not about.
Mara I'll talk to you, love.
Owen Then give me that.
Mara Tomorrow.
Owen Now.

He snatches at the pages in her hand, and they tear

Oh God. I've torn it.
Mara It doesn't matter.

Owen This is your work, Mara!
Mara It's nothing.
Owen It's you! This is you I've torn!
Mara I don't mind, love.
Owen Oh God.
Mara I don't care how you use me.
Owen Oh God oh God oh God oh God.
Mara I'm no-one. I'm nothing.
Owen No! I want *you* to use *me*!
Mara I don't want to use you, love.
Owen Make any use you can of me. Turn me into words.
Mara I want you, love, not words.
Owen I'm nothing, except as you see me.
Mara Let's go now.
Owen Walk. The canefields.
Mara Before the clouds burst.
Owen (*picking up the torn pages*) Put this together again.
Mara Later.
Owen Copy it. I'll copy it.
Mara Only words.
Owen Hurt us like stones.
Mara No more words.
Owen (*reading*) "I do," he said. "I do. I do."
Mara (*gently*) Don't. (*She tries to take the page away from him*)
Owen "I do. I do. I do. I do."
Mara Well, you do.
Owen (*sadly*) You were writing it down even as I was saying it.
Mara You do love her.
Owen Taking it at dictation.
Mara You do say it, too.
Owen And you note it down as if I were holding a press conference.
Mara No. It's what you said before.
Owen I said it just then! While you were writing!
Mara You also said it before.
Owen When?
Mara This afternoon.
Owen Where?
Mara Behind the kitchens at the rural medical centre.

Owen Then? I said that in agony!
Mara Also yesterday, at the fertilizer plant.
Owen You make it sound as if I'm saying it all the time!
Mara You *are* saying it all the time!
Owen I don't say "I do, I do, I do" six times in a row!
Mara You do!
Owen You mean you counted?
Mara I counted!
Owen You counted. And then you carefully wrote it down.
Mara You gave me a lecture once on getting quotations down accurately.
Owen I didn't mean to write reports on *me*!
Mara I simply wrote down what you said! Your own words! How can that be wrong?
Owen Are you honestly trying to tell me that you have never heard of a statement being made *off the record*?

Hilberto enters. He sits down on the chairs at the back and watches them

Mara Are you trying to tell me that was a *confidential briefing*?
Owen Of course it was confidential!
Mara *Not for attribution?*
Owen Do I have to stamp it over everything I say to you?

Mara laughs

Don't you laugh at me!
Mara (*furiously*) I *will* laugh at you!
Owen (*furiously*) All right, then, I shall laugh at *you*!
Mara Go ahead, then! Laugh!
Owen *You* laugh!
Mara I want to hear *you* laugh first!
Owen You were the one who wanted to laugh!

Mara bursts into tears

That's right! Cry!

Mara gathers up her papers

Owen Now what? Now where are you going? I thought we were going to the canefields?

Mara laughs angrily through her tears, and hurries off

Owen smashes his fist down on the table

God! Talk about changing your mind!

He sees Hilberto. Hilberto moves his head from side to side in sympathy. Owen gestures with his arms and eyebrows to indicate the impossibility of the situation. Hilberto points to the plaster on his face. Owen nods. Thunder. Hilberto indicates the sky, and demonstrates wiping his brow. Owen nods. He sits down at the table and slumps across it, exhausted. Hilberto takes a cigar out of his shirt pocket and offers it to him. Owen sits up

But she's so . . . *unprofessional*!

The foreground Lights go down. The sky becomes completely black. Sheet lightning flickers dimly

SCENE 7

The chairs are arranged as for the five separate illuminated areas in Scene 4 of this act. But only one of the five areas is illuminated. In it, Angel sits on the raised level that serves as his bed. His head is sunk in his hands. A bottle of rum stands on his chair

Thunder

Angel stirs, and takes a drink from the bottle. A click, and the Light in Mara's area comes on. She is standing there, still holding her papers. She sits down on her "bed". Her head sinks into her hands. She sobs. Angel lifts his head and listens. Another click. The Light in Ed's area comes on. He is lying on his bed. He sits up and listens. Mara sobs. Angel's head and Ed's head both sink into their hands. Click. The Light comes on in Owen's area, and Owen is standing there. He sits down on his bed. His head sinks into his hands. A rumble of thunder. Mara sobs. Angel crosses to Mara's area, and stands looking at her. She hides her head at his approach, and keeps it hidden. Owen and Ed lift their heads and listen

Angel Bravo! Encore! (*He claps*) Bravo! Bravo! And they laugh.

They laugh and they laugh. They put their arms round the man in spectacles who plays the maraccas, and they say, "See how handsome he is!" They make my father sit down, and they give him drinks, and they say, "We love you!" And I sit there, where no-one sees me. And I watch them. I watch them. Exactly so as now I sit here each day and watch you and Mr Shorter. You put your arm round me, exactly so as they put their arm round the man with the maraccas. "Oh, Angel, you are sweet!" And you say it exactly so, as when they give my father money, and pour him rum. "Oh, Angel, we love this country!" And you say it exactly so, as when they shout out, "Bravo! Encore!" And I sit here, inside myself where no-one can see me. And I watch you. I watch you.

Mara (*lifting her head*) Angel, I'm not laughing now.

Angel Yes, I think now you are sad again.

Mara Don't you hate me, too.

Angel Yes, now you speak to me again so.

Mara Don't you look at me with hard eyes.

Angel One day you speak to me so, and the next day you laugh.

Mara I only laughed because I was happy.

Angel "Oh, Angel, you are sweet!"

Mara Angel . . .

Angel "Oh, Angel, we love this country!"

Mara Angel . . .

Angel And they laughed. At my father, at my people. And what I cannot forget is this: I also laughed.

He sits beside her, head in hands. She puts her arm round him

I laughed with them.

Mara We won't laugh any more, Angel. Now we'll both cry. For each other. And for ourselves.

Owen crosses to Mara's area

Owen Of course! (*He laughs bitterly*) Of course!

Angel I think you must go away, please.

Owen Military installation, is it?

Mara I think you'd better go.

Owen laughs furiously

Angel I think you must not laugh.
Owen Mustn't *laugh*?
Mara I think definitely not laugh.
Owen Well, I'm going to laugh. There may be no freedom of speech here, but there must be freedom of laughter! I'm going to stand here and laugh and laugh and laugh until edition time!

He laughs. Angel stands up and hits him. Owen stops laughing in amazement

You hit me.
Angel I hit you, yes.
Owen I don't believe it!
Angel I think I hit you also again.
Owen Never—*never*—in twenty years in this trade have I been hit by a public relations officer!

Angel hits him again. Mara runs to Ed's area

Mara They're going to kill each other!

Mara and Ed return to Mara's area

Owen You hit me again! (*To Ed*) He hit me! This man hit me!
Ed Owen—Angel—if you could see yourselves, you'd laugh.
Owen He actually *hit* me! (*To Angel*) I'm going to hit you. Do you realize that? I'm going to hit you very hard.
Angel Hit me.
Ed *No le provoques.*
Angel Hit me.
Owen I *shall* hit you, don't worry.
Angel Hit me. Hit me.
Owen I'm *going* to hit you.

Angel hits Owen

You hit *me!*
Ed (*lays a hand on each of them*) Stop! Stop! Stop! What's this about? Will someone please enlighten me?

Total Black-out. Thunder. Mara cries out. The Lights come on again

Mara What happened?
Angel I think the storm affects the electricity.
Owen A power-failure! What else?

Owen laughs hysterically. Angel moves to attack him again. Ed prevents him

Ed No! It's all over. No more. Relax. Everything's back to normal.

Total Black-out. Owen laughs hysterically again. The laughter ends suddenly in a cry of pain. The scene is illuminated briefly by lightning. It reveals a tableau vivant *in which everyone is as before, except that Owen is doubled up in agony. Music begins—a cha-cha-cha*

Darkness

More lightning. Another tableau, this time revealing Owen holding the chair above his head, ready to bring it down upon Angel. Ed with peacemaking hands ineffectually raised

Darkness. Mara screams

Lightning. Tableau: Owen with chair brought down upon the floor, and Angel escaped to the other side of him. Ed in peacemaking role

Darkness

Lightning. Tableau: Owen has now brought the chair down upon the spot where Angel was standing in the last tableau. Angel has shifted round behind him and is holding a chair of his own upraised to strike. Ed peacemaking. No sign of Mara

Darkness

Lightning. Tableau: Angel and Owen have both brought their chairs together. They have felled Ed, who is lying on the floor trying to protect himself

Darkness

Angel Mara!
Owen Mara!

Lightning. Tableau: Ed on the floor. Owen and Angel, chairs thrown down, searching outwards

Darkness

Owen Mara!

Angel (*fainter*) Mara!
Owen (*fainter still*) Mara! Mara!

Lightning. Tableau: Ed is sitting up holding his head

Darkness

Lightning. Tableau: Ed is huddled on the floor again. No Owen. No Angel. Mara and Hilberto are gazing at the motionless Ed

Darkness

Lightning. Tableau: Ed, as before. Mara, having turned away from the sight of Ed, has taken refuge in Hilberto's arms. Hilberto is looking surprised

Darkness. Torrential rain

Scene 8

Car and sky. The sky is pure blue

Hilberto is driving. Mara sits next to him. In the back sit Angel, Owen and Ed. Ed's head is bandaged; Owen is wearing dark glasses; Angel has a patch over one eye. All three are in low spirits

Mara Oh, the air! The air! So cool. So new. How strange that you can feel it round your face and in your lungs like that, when there's nothing there to be seen. Pure weightlessness. Pure transparency. Pure emptiness. On a morning like this there are no distances. Everything's hard and sharp and unambiguous. You can see raindrops sparkling on the leaves of trees a mile and more off. You can see the shape of the palm leaves on palm leaf cabins high up on the mountainside. You can see the oranges on the wild orange-trees, and the red berries of wild coffee. Every breath you take is sharp and chill, and full of oranges and raindrops. Every breath you take, you draw wild coffee and blue sky into your lungs and blood. The world's beginning again; and this time round it's going to be a very different story. (*She turns and looks at the three in the back*) Breathe it in! Breathe, breathe, breathe! Don't just sit there thinking about your troubles! Everything's going to be all right. Angel, don't worry about that eye. We'll get it looked at as soon as we get back to Havana.

Angel looks away

Ed, do you want another aspirin?

Ed shakes his head, then holds it

I shouldn't shake it, if I were you. It doesn't hurt to speak, does it?

Ed holds his jaw, and nods, then holds his head again

Mara I shouldn't nod it, either. Just sit still and enjoy the air.

Owen shivers

Owen, don't keep shivering like that. You can't have got influenza that quickly.

Owen shivers

Well, you should have looked properly in the hotel first. It was ridiculous to run out without looking in the middle of a cloudburst. It was absurd to spend half the night searching for me in the canefields. Why the canefields? And why didn't you stop to put some clothes on first?

Owen shivers

I think you'd feel better if you'd had some breakfast. There wasn't anything left by the time you got up, was there?

Owen Mango-juice.

Mara picks up the instrument lying on the seat between her and Hilberto

Mara Anyway, I'm very pleased with my ophthalmoscope. No-one's ever given me an ophthalmoscope before.

Hilberto grins

Look at that old boy on the donkey! Big cigar! Sitting back, looking as if he owned the place!

Hilberto Whee—heeeee!

Mara And look at this old boy in the Cadillac! Also looking very content with life!

Hilberto Whee—heeeee!

Mara And look at that sky. Not a cloud in sight. Pure light. Pure emptiness. Everything.

CURTAIN